PENGUIN BOOKS

The Rights of Man

H. G. Wells (1866–1946) was a professional writer and journalist who published more than a hundred books, including pioneering science fiction novels, histories, essays and programmes for world regeneration.

He was a founding member of numerous movements including Liberty and PEN International – the world's oldest human rights organization – and his *Rights of Man* laid the groundwork for the 1948 Universal Declaration of Human Rights. Wells's controversial and progressive views on equality and the shape of a truly developed nation remain directly relevant to our world today.

Ali Smith was born in Inverness in 1962 and lives in Cambridge. Her latest novel, *How to be both*, won the Bailey's Women's Prize for Fiction, the Costa Novel of the Year and the Goldsmith's Prize, and was shortlisted for the Man Booker and the Folio Prize. Her latest story collection is *Public library and other stories*.

THE RIGHTS OF MAN

Or What Are We Fighting For?

H. G. Wells

With an introduction by Ali Smith

PUBLISHED AS A 'PENGUIN SPECIAL' BY
PENGUIN BOOKS LIMITED
80 STRAND LONDON ENGLAND

PENGUIN BOOKS

UK | USA | Canada | Ireland | Australia
India | New Zealand | South Africa

Penguin Books is part of the Penguin Random House group of companies
whose addresses can be found at global.penguinrandomhouse.com.

First published as a Penguin Special 1940
Reissued with a new introduction in Penguin Books 2015

001

'What Are We Fighting For?' copyright © Ali Smith, 2015

The moral right of the copyright holders has been asserted

Set in 11.6/15 pt Fournier MT Std
Typeset by Jouve (UK), Milton Keynes
Printed in Great Britain by Clays Ltd, St Ives plc

A CIP catalogue record for this book is available from the British Library

ISBN: 978–0–241–97676–0

www.greenpenguin.co.uk

Contents

What Are We Fighting For?

The 2nd Annual PEN H. G. Wells Lecture, 15 August 2015

Ali Smith

'These people were two hundred years further on in the march of civilisation than the Victorian generation. It was not likely they would be less – humane.'

H. G. Wells, When the Sleeper Wakes, *1899*

I was sitting in the café of a theatre in London waiting to go in to see a new play about cloning. The play was rather mysterious, or rather, the process of getting in to see it was. On my ticket there wasn't a seat number, there was just a number. Number 103. What does this mean? I'd asked the man at the box office. It means you're number 103, the man said.

I checked my phone, which is what I use now, like so many of us, instead of a watch. There were forty-five minutes before the doors. I sat down and took my book out of my bag. Ann Veronica. 1909. H. G. Wells.

I was spending quite a lot of my days in this very recent past worrying about a lecture that I was going to have to give in Edinburgh in the too near future. I had no idea yet what it would be about. It was in honour of Wells, I knew a bit about him, I knew a great deal vicariously – I'd seen the films, knew the tropes – but had read very little *by* him, though I knew what we all knew, that he'd written several of the most seminal visionary texts not just of the past century or so, but ever, and he'd been world-famous, hugely so in his time, and deeply politically engaged, and very very human, it sounded like, with so many extramarital lovers that his social and amorous peccadilloes were an open joke among some of the more aesthetically experimental writers alive at the same time as him about whom and by whom, because of the way my life had taken its shape, I happened to have read much more. I'd hardly read him though, and he'd written a hundred – more than a hundred – books, and me supposed to be so well read etc. – and the lecture was relatively soon, and though it could really be about anything and didn't have to be about Wells, I had decided to read as much by him as I could in the time I had and see what happened. Ann Veronica. 1909. Page 1. Chapter 1. Ann Veronica Talks to Her Father.

It was about a spirited young woman on the edge of her seat on a train, determined to make a future for herself different from the one that's expected and permitted. She lives in the suburbs and is on her way home right now to have a blazing argument with her father about how she wants to live her life and do what she wants regardless of what he wants; she's bright, and full of kick and spirit, all coiled energy, life and impetus, and the question all through the prose is: can such energy be contained?

She wanted to live. She was vehemently impatient – she did not clearly know for what – to do, to be, to experience. And experience was slow in coming. All the world about her seemed to be – how can one put it – in wrappers, like a house when people leave it in the summer. The blinds were all drawn, the sunlight kept out, one could not tell what colours these grey swathings hid. She wanted to know. And there was no intimation whatever that –

But I couldn't concentrate, because of the man sitting next to me, who was holding forth to a young woman he was with about his Watch. They were both in their late twenties, maybe early thirties. Were they together? It was hard to tell, she was sitting opposite saying almost nothing while he told her how many steps he'd taken that day, how many minutes in the hour had been exercise minutes compared to the number of minutes when he'd been sitting down, he'd done two hours and forty-three minutes of exercise today so far, and then he detailed the difference between the exercise minutes which were moving-about minutes and the minutes in each hour he'd merely stood for, he'd been standing rather than sitting, according to his particular time machine, for three to four minutes in every hour. Which was apparently a really good standing-for statistic, he said.

I carried on pretending to read my book and sur-reptitiously glanced at the young woman. I was wondering how much longer *she'd* stand for much more of this stunningly boring self-mythologizing. But she was nodding and saying nothing, so I started worrying that maybe this was now the new chat-up routine, and that maybe I'd become dated myself not to know that this was what passed, in a different generation, for a display of prowess. *Choose me, I stand for an average of three minutes and forty-seven seconds in every sixty minutes.* Anyway, she and I, both, had to stand literally about twenty more minutes of what the Watch had told him about himself, before I looked at my phone and saw it was time to find out what number 103, my number, meant, and closed my unread book.

The play was good. It was by Caryl Churchill, and called A Number. She's one of our visionaries right now, and her vision of the future, and of the tragedy of the lost original self in all the multiple selves we're capable of, meant I didn't open my book on the train home, I just sat and stared out the window, thinking about the games people play with real lives in the real world. Then I began to worry again about all the work I had to do, real catch-up work reading one of the original modern visionaries, and when I got home I still didn't open the book but distracted myself instead thinking about the word watch. I began wondering why watches had been called watches, and what watching had to do with time, and vice versa, how time was related to the word watch, and to notions of watching.

I looked up the etymology of watch. Verb, transitive. To follow the motions of with the eyes. To observe the progress of, maintain an interest in. To have in one's care, to look after, to guard, to tend. To beware of danger to or from, to be on the alert to take advantage of. To wait for. To catch in the act. To keep a hawk from sleep in order to tame it (those last two are Shakespearian uses). To look with attention. To remain awake. To keep vigil. To attend the sick by night. Noun. A small timepiece for wearing on a strap round the wrist or carrying in a pocket. The state of being, or act of staying, awake. A religious vigil. A vigil beside a corpse, a wake. The collective noun for a flock of nightingales. A division of the night. The dark hours of the night. Close observation. Surveillance. The body of men who, before the institution of a police force, patrolled the streets at night. The name applied to certain companies of irregular troops in the Scottish Highlands. From the Old English waecce, waeccan, wacian, from wacan, to wake.

I wrote it down. It'd no doubt be useful. Beyond me, the news was on the TV screen. It was about how the government was going to shelve its plans to scrap the Human Rights Act and replace it with a British bill of rights for the moment, because they couldn't yet be sure of having enough support to see their dismantlement plan safely through Parliament. They were going to work on raising the support. Then it was about the number of migrants who'd died in the sea last year compared to the number who'd died in the sea so far this year. Two thousand dead in the Med, the announcer said, just like that, like it rhymed. Two hundred thousand picked up already this year. Last year, a hundred and seventy thousand.

The migrants who die and the migrants who survive, whether they survive or they die, are always described like that, a number. They are never allowed to be the individuals each person, dead or alive, actually is. It's like we're meant to think of migrants, according to the media, like clones, like each migrant is not a person, just a 'migrant'. I started worrying about that instead, then went, as if programmed, to the surface worry easiest to have right then in my life, the H. G. Wells book still closed in my bag, the pile of waiting books on the table that went towering way up over my head.

It was half past one in the morning. Instead of reading, or sleeping, I decided to ask Google about looking into the future. I typed into the search box the words: HOW TO LOOK INTO. That's as far as I got before THE FUTURE came up by itself, in that predictive box that shows us the most asked questions with the same wording on Google. But below that, the rest of what people ask when they ask Google *how to look into* caught my eye.

It read like a little poem:

> *How to look into the future*
> *how to look into someone's eyes*
> *how to look into someone's phone*
> *how to look into your icloud*
> *how to look into private instagram accounts*
> *how to look into the camera*

how to look into your ear
how to look into yourself
how to look into someone's whatsapp
how to look into a jar file

Our contemporary looking is closely bound up with the usual age-old human concerns but also some very new ones. We want to know, as ever, what's going to happen to us before it does, and how to go about intimacy – but now also how to bypass others' privacy. We want to know how best to be seen and recorded, how best to see ourselves – and how to work the technologies that are these days working on and giving out versions of us.

I clicked on the top one, *the future*. Up came all manner of sites. Numerology, astrology, stichomancy, computer programs which flush out patterns, statistical analysis for financial and sports predictions, animal entrails-reading, Nostradamus, crystal balls, the automated death-clock which will help you predict, if you enter your health details, the exact date of your death, and that site too where if you upload a picture of yourself it will let you 'see yourself in 20 years' – by making the face fatter and shading in areas so the person in the future looks really ill.

I clicked on a site called Sunangel.com. There was

a lilac-coloured graphic of a door. It said ASK FORTUNA on it, and the word ask was above a large doorknob. Next to it, it said: *The Goddess Fortuna bestows protection, prosperity, success and good luck to all those who believe in the magic of joyful intentions! The ancient Romans believed in her power to transform their lives, so why don't we ask her for a little guidance? Sit back and relax. Let your mind quietly and gently focus on your question. When the feeling is right, ask Fortuna for your message from the Universe.*

I sat back and relaxed. What will my H. G. Wells lecture be about? I asked Fortuna in my head. I clicked on the doorknob. A graphic of a Pre-Raphaelite wispy-clothed angelic-looking lady in the clouds appeared in an open doorway, and next to her the words said: *Fortuna's answer: There is invisible support all around you.* How lovely. How reassuring. It also said, below this, ASK AGAIN.

I sat back again and relaxed again. But how exactly will this invisible support help me with writing my H. G. Wells lecture? I asked, and clicked on the doorknob. *Fortuna's answer: There is invisible support all around you.*

I asked a couple more times, and I asked a couple of different questions, and clicked, each time, on the door-knob. Each time: *Fortuna's answer: There is invisible support all around you.*

Ask Fortuna. Ask for tuna. The future for tuna was pretty fishy for sure. And invisible. But supportive. I went to bed. I fell asleep.

I woke up with a start, because someone was talking in the dark in my room. It was quite a high-pitched voice, hissing like an old radio recording.

I see no reason why a man should live like a brute because he knows of nothing beyond matter, and does not expect to exist a hundred years hence. That's 1896. Short story. *A Slip Under the Microscope.* A chap inadvertently cheats at an exam. But then can't live with himself and ruins his life by telling the authorities. Moral biology.

I sat up. There was a figure at the end of the bed.

The uglier a man's legs are, the better he plays golf. It's almost a law. 1915. From *Bealby*.

What? I said.

Every time I see an adult on a bicycle, I no longer despair for the future of the human race, the figure said.

Who are you? I said.

I'm – I'm a Visitant from Another World. And that's from near the end of History of Mr Polly, *1910. Sold thousands.* You read it yourself, in another world. Remember? You were sixteen. Parents had demanded you stay at home because of visitors coming. So you sat in the front room with them and the visitors and you read the book openly and ignored them all. Remember yet?

It was true, forty years ago, me sitting in the front room holding the book between me and the visitors like a little shield, a proof that I had a life beyond this life. I'd wanted to go to Edinburgh to see The Clash. I'd been made to stay at home ostensibly because visitors were coming round, largely because Edinburgh was hundreds of miles away and there would be boys going. I'd sat in the front room and held the book up between me and everything to display my disdain. '"Hole!" said Mr Polly, and then for a change, and with greatly increased emphasis: "'Ole!"' Look at me back there, as if it were now and no future has happened yet, standing in Melvens, our local bookshop, reading the opening lines of a book I've taken off a shelf by chance, The History of Mr Polly by H. G. Wells, about a man sitting on a stile between some 'threadbare looking fields' and trying out the difference between received pronunciation and accent, between what a word should be and what a word is, word on the page versus word in the mouth, the gap between the given word and your own voice.

It was as if his soul had been cramped and his eyes band-aged from the hour of his birth. Why had he lived such a life? Why had he submitted to things, blundered into things? Why had he never insisted on the things he thought beautiful and the things he desired, never sought them, fought for them, taken any risk for them, died rather than abandon them? They were the things that mattered. Safety did not matter. A living did not matter unless there were things to live for.

I knew it, the paragraph, sort of by heart. It had struck home with me, at sixteen.

I switched the bedside light on. The figure at the end of the bed was thin, looked starved, had a young man's figure and face, soulful blue eyes, a little thin moustache – though it looked as if someone had coloured the face in, shadowed it with areas of digital dark overlay so that it looked much much older, and shifted as I watched, was at the same time an old and balding portly man's face.

Pre-cognitive dream, he said.

Oh, I said.

I never talk for broadcasting without a real live listener actually in the room with me. I said that in The English Speaking World as I See It, 1937. And here's another you'll like, from that same talk. Nothing can pull our minds together as powerfully as books.

But he'd begun to fade, there at the end of my bed, so that I could see the room through the arm he was holding out as he spoke, then through his torso I could see the mirror opposite the bed and me in it, though the voice wasn't fading, it was still as strange and high and strong as the voice that had wakened me.

I was never a great amorist, though I have loved several people very deeply. That's from *Experiment in Autobiography, 1934. And: Our true nationality is mankind. Yes?*

Yes, I said.

The Outline of History, 1920, he said.

He was completely invisible now, there was nothing in the room but the words in the voice.

And: listening? What a wonderfully complex thing! this simple seeming unity — the self! Who can trace its reintegration as morning after morning we awaken, the flux and confluence of its countless factors interweaving, rebuilding, the dim first stirrings of the soul, the growth and synthesis of the unconscious to the subconscious, the subconscious to dawning consciousness, until at last we recognise ourselves again. 1899. When the Sleeper Wakes.

I opened my eyes. I sat up. There was no one in the room. Obviously.

Fast-forward a couple of weeks. I'm sitting in the car waiting for my friend so we can drive home from Suffolk. She's gone into an old church to have a look at the past. She's got a copy of Pevsner with her and is taking photos of some age-old violences, Reformation damage to the carved angels' faces and the blackened scraped-off burnt-off faces of saints and apostles painted on the church's wooden screen. Anyway I'm sitting waiting, car door open because it's so warm, and I'm reading about another kind of facelessness in The Invisible Man, far and away my favourite of the Wells novels I've read so far.

I now know a lot more than I used to about his life. His parents owned a shop in Bromley, Atlas House it was called, selling china and cricket bats. Cricket bat in a china shop! – his father had been a cricket professional. But the shop wasn't a roaring success and it was in a world of comparative poverty and illness that the young Wells grew up, and after his father broke a leg the shop closed, the family fell apart and his mother went back to lady's-maiding at a big house in Suffolk, which her son often sneaked into the library of and read as much as he could get away with. He remembers, in his autobiography, his youth as a hungry one, a malnourished one. Nourishment, and what it is, and hunger as a theme, and how we are what we eat, run through all his books from The Time Machine onwards. Economic pressure meant the family's kids all went into apprenticeships; his was as a draper's assistant, from which he managed to escape into trainings in both teaching and biology – his first book was Text-Book of Biology, 1893. The biologist became an early uniter of those seeming opposites, art and science, when he began writing serials which went into book form and the new reading masses were quick to take him to their hearts, and in two to three years the young man, just turned thirty, had produced not just an astonishing four novels, but four that were classics as soon as published, and still are. The Time Machine. The Island of Doctor Moreau. The Invisible Man. The War of the Worlds.

As the new century opened he wrote futuristic essays and political tracts, and then alongside these and his novels of the fantastic, the 'scientific romances', he developed a self-satirizing form of the socio-realist novel. He was prolific and popular. As the new century continued he became what a writer like Virginia Woolf called a celebrity.

Woolf and Wells knew each other first because Leonard Woolf and H. G. Wells were both members of the League of Nations, which Wells had helped to set up. She knew him through his PEN presidency, which he held from 1933 to 1935; he'd been an early member of the group, the role of which was to promote friendship and intellectual cooperation among writers everywhere. Wells had also been deeply involved – in 1934, after the callous treatment of the Hunger Marchers by the police and by Parliament – in the formation of the National Council for Civil Liberties, now known as Liberty. (Of both PEN and Liberty more later, and of his 1940 political tract, The Rights of Man, the book which meant he was instrumental very late in his life, and even after his death, in the setting up and drafting of every one of our international human rights acts and declarations.)

Right now, some weeks ago, in July 2015, I'm sitting in the car outside the old church reading The Invisible Man; back then, in July 1935, Virginia Woolf is writing to her sister Vanessa Bell hilariously, archly and acidly, about turning down, herself, the offer of the presidency of the PEN Club after Wells: 'I have been asked to be President of the P.E.N. Club in succession to Wells: this is about the greatest insult that could be offered a writer, or a human being.' An 'inky little podgy under-world man' has come to see her to offer her this presidency and it is beyond her to imagine what use such a presidency could be, or what use she could be to it. It's easy to make fun of activism – in the UK as a whole we've never had a culture that's understood, or forgiven, the potency of the activist; we've hardly ever forgiven our intellectuals as it is; Wells was always a little too jingoist for Woolf, and maybe she was keen to avoid the kind of stand Wells had had to take at PEN just the year before, excluding German PEN from PEN's international organization, for its own violent excluding behaviour towards Jewish writers and writers of other-than-Nazi political belief. Wells's own books had gone up in flames as 'anti-German' in the notorious performances of book-burning in 1933, and Wells had been a protector of Ernst Toller's right to speak at a PEN conference in Italy regardless of the Nazi attempts to have him and other anti-Nazi voices suppressed.

Meetings between writers are always fraught with the politics of their times, because writers, to paraphrase the great Nobel Prize-winner José Saramago, can't not be political simply by dint of being human and being citizens. This does not mean that written works will be propagandist. But it means written works have eyes. They're able to see, and reveal what they see. They're able to watch. The word Saramago favours is observe.

Woolf was also, like us all, helplessly a creature of her time. Here's how helplessly politically she saw Wells, the self-made grown-old man, in her diary. She tells him jokingly she thinks Americans 'alien to our civilisation. He said he had been that himself. His father was a gardener, his mother a ladies maid. He found it very strange to meet people who went to parties & wore dress clothes.' In the dark of January 1937, in a time rolling on inexorably towards the future, sensed but as yet unknown – invisible still those even darker times and her name and her husband's name in the alphabetical list of people to be summarily arrested in the pages of the Black Book of the Nazis, and H. G. Wells's name in there too – she spends a pleasant, judgemental evening in the company of Wells the celebrity:

[his] old man's talk; mellower than I remembered; mischievous; eyes a little bleared; kindly in his way; merry . . . conscious of his lack of distinction; prone to snap at any pretence; introduced, 'my father the professional cricketer'; content I think with his position, & immensely interested still. He wished to live to be 170. is 70 . . . And I suspect that when he faces his Trinity at dead of night there are a good many books that he thinks justly, trash: & he shuffles his hands among the loose innumerable pages . . . remembers that he has done a vast mass of work, & thinks it wont all die; & is amused at the place he has made – from Bromley Kent to Regents Park . . . & I suppose the greatest circulation in the whole world. A humane man in some corner; also brutal; also entirely without poetry.

This I scribble with the snow darkening my skylight . . .

The glorious Woolf could be cold and pretty brutal herself (though rarely without poetry) – maybe some of her coolness here is because Wells, over the years, had regularly left her out of his round-up of talented younger writers, and had told her husband once, years back, that she was 'too intelligent – a bad thing'. She abhorred his take on 'the role of women in the world's work' – and yes, this is him too, sitting pompously on the edge of Woolf's bed, or my bed, all the women's beds, holding forth in 1932: *Hitherto the role of women has been decorative and ancillary. And today it seems to be still decorative and ancillary . . . her recent gains in freedom have widened her choice of what she shall adorn or serve, but they have released no new initiative in human affairs.* He was, as human beings are, mistaken and messy about lots of things. It's worth remembering here his fashionable support, early in the century, of eugenics, which Joseph Conrad, in a letter to him, roundly told him off about, though it's worth remembering here too how that notion of lesser beings central to eugenics is always coming in and out of fashion in various disguises. You'd have thought we'd have grown out of it by now, but look at the way our own statesmen, government and press are dealing with the 'swarm' – a word which just this morning, on the hundredth day of his government, David Cameron has reiterated, saying people *will know what he means* when he uses it – the 'swarm', the 'organized mob', the 'unstoppable flood' of human beings each with his or her own inaudible voice, who have been uprooted by war, or genocide, or tyranny, or exploit-ation (because nobody leaves home unless he or she has to), people who need help and safe haven. More about our governmental xenophobia and moral immaturity later, and back to H. G. Wells's believing naively that the 1914 war-to-end-all-wars maybe wouldn't be a bad thing, since it would do away with nationalisms and divides between people. He lived and learned. His ideal-isms fluctuated and matured. I know mine have, over the years, but with any luck I'm learning; we all do a bit of time-travelling, with any luck.

And in her essays Virginia Woolf treats Wells much more charmingly if no less caustically: she comments on how he 'fills us with his generous enthusiasm'. She can't deny the verve and the life in him: 'he throws off the trammels of fiction,' she writes, 'as lightly as he would throw off a coat in running a race.' Here's what H. G. Wells thought about the notion of running a race. *Human history becomes more and more a race between edu-cation and catastrophe.* Woolf, of course, was fighting fiercely for a new future for all of us too, via a different kind of space travel – the space of a room of one's own. Wells wanted something else altogether: *I am extremely obsessed by the thing that might be, and impatient with the present; I want to go ahead of Father Time with a scythe of my own.*

And here, ten years ago in 2005, is another great novelist, one who's learned equally from both Woolf and Wells, Margaret Atwood. In her introduction for an edition of The Island of Doctor Moreau, she writes specifically about Wells and class with an open eye to how Wells sliced through his own history:

> To some of literature's more gentlemanly practitioners – those, for instance, who had inherited money, and didn't have to make it by scribbling – Wells must have seemed like a puffed-up little counter-jumper, and a challenging one at that, because he was bright. He'd come up the hard way.

Back to me sitting in the car, reading The Invisible Man and marvelling at how good Wells is at writing about the very real grime and dirt of the city at the end of the nineteenth and the beginning of the twentieth century, dirt being one of the things that make an invisible man visible:

> as I went abroad – in the London air – I gathered dirt about my ankles, floating smuts and dust upon my skin. I did not know how long it would be before I should become visible . . . I saw clearly it could not be for long.

I'm reading the novel with the car radio on so I can keep an eye on the time, it's 2 p.m. and the Radio 4 news comes on. The Israeli government is planning to make stone-throwing an act of terrorism punishable by twenty years in prison. A left-wing UK politician vying for leadership is telling everyone he abstained from voting against the government and austerity as an act of solidarity and keeping the Labour Party together, but that really underneath it all he's very left wing. And, according to the Home Office, asylum seekers with children are going to be stripped of benefits in order to send a message to migrants in Calais that Britain is not a 'land of milk and honey', and landlords are going to be imprisoned if they find themselves letting to illegal immigrants.

Terrorism. Stone-throwing, by those small boys who throw stones at the tanks that are flattening their homes. I spend a lot of time these days staring in disbelief at the radio, the TV, the computer screen. What can I do about it? What can I do about anything?

This is H. G. Wells, invisible but there anyway thank God, in the back of the car and the back of the mind, at the back of the twentieth century, in 1916 and writing in a book called What is Coming?: *I hate and despise a shrewish suspicion of foreigners and foreign ways;*

a man who can look me in the face, laugh with me, speak truth and deal fairly, is my brother. And in the book open in my hands, The Invisible Man has just proved his existence by throwing little stones through the air at another of society's outcasts, or invisibles, a tramp sitting in a ditch, a man called Thomas Marvel. The tramp thinks he's imagining things, hearing voices, because he's had a few:

> 'I'm going to throw flints at you till you think differently.' . . .
>
> Whizz came a flint, apparently out of the air, and missed Mr Marvel's shoulder by a hair's breadth. Mr Marvel, turning, saw a flint jerk up into the air, trace a complicated path, hang for a moment, and then fall at his feet with almost invisible rapidity. He was too amazed to dodge. Whizz it came, and ricocheted from a bare toe into the ditch. Mr Marvel jumped a foot and howled aloud . . .
>
> '*Now*,' said the Voice, as a third stone curved upward and hung in the air above the tramp. 'Am I imagination?'

I have already myself been marvelling at the way in which Wells has pre-found a vehicle or device for expression for all the outcasts, all the people and peoples who feel or are rendered invisible; this is maybe most directly and indebtedly expressed in Ralph Ellison's seminal novel written more than half a century later and called Invisible Man. Ellison will have known this passage on page 20 of Wells's 1897 novel, where a local man is, with a casual inhumanity, trying to explain to another that he knows what the mysterious bandaged-faced man who's just moved into the local pub looks like under his bandages – and how he knows is because his dog has bitten the man:

> 'Well, he's black. Leastways, his legs are. I seed through the tear of his trousers and the tear of his glove. You'd have expected a sort of pinky to show, wouldn't you? Well – there wasn't none. Just blackness.'

That's just one of the pre-seeings in Wells's fiction. Here's a random list of just some of the things Wells foretells in his work, usually decades before these things were real or thought possible, many of them now norms to us. Tanks : global warming : the ethical and physical questions about vivisection : aerial flight in heavier-than-air aeroplane form – he writes about it some years before Orville and Wilbur Wright actually do it, and knows when it comes it'll be for leisure but also for bombardment : the vision of the floating astronauts and their floating belongings in their capsules on their way to the moon : visible mass surveillance : invisible mass surveillance : modern germ warfare : radio, TV, video : the World Wide Web – he called it the 'world encyclopaedia' and saw it as a sure way to win that historic race between education and catastrophe.

His first novel, The Time Machine, was all about split worlds, and in it he points out a split between the social classes caused and maintained by who has access to education and who hasn't. He'd become keen, as he matured, on a meritocratic World State, and in the last decade of his life his notion of a 'world brain', that world encyclopaedia, stood for a democratic and internationally wide-open education. 'The time is close at hand,' he wrote, 'when any student, in any part of the world, will be able to sit with his projector in his own study at his or her convenience to examine *any* book, *any* document.' There it is, that resource, on a screen near you – in your hand – on your Watch, if you like. It's up to us how we use the World Brain.

More: he foresaw European union : invasion of privacy : the political or power-driven implementation of mass and cultural panic for others' gain : drones : the atom bomb : fallout : radioactive waste : modern chemical weaponry : the modern underclass : the rise of suburbia : laser beams : mandatory identity cards and surveillance techniques 'by which every person in the world can be promptly and certainly recognised' : cosmetic surgery : a rise in sexual freedoms for both genders : the shift away from newspapers to screens and away from written materials and letter-writing by hand : the ubiquity and vivacity of the tramp figure long before Chaplin embodied him for the world.

And here is Wells talking about rewriting When the Sleeper Wakes a decade later and tweaking the future a little with the addition of *higher buildings, bigger towns, wickeder capitalists and labour more downtrodden than ever and more desperate. Everything was bigger, quicker and more crowded; there was more and more flying and the wildest financial speculation.* Sound familiar? In this dystopic book, a man falls asleep in Victorian times and wakes up just over two hundred years later to a 'nightmare of Capitalism triumphant' and to be told he's the 'Master of the Earth . . . owner of the world' – but that actually what he 'owns' belongs to a controlling elite who've been investing it in their own interest and running an underclass slavery system with it. His references, in the 1890s, to the War, or Wars, seem uncanny now, even if the wars he's talking about are fantastical invented ones. In The War of the Worlds, 1898, discussion of the uses of trench warfare is now also uncannily framed by aftermath. He even foresaw Dalí or de Chirico, in The Invisible Man, in this vision the innkeeper's wife has after encountering the invisible man: 'in the middle of the night she woke up dreaming of huge white heads like turnips, that came trailing after her at the end of interminable necks, and with vast black eyes.'

The Invisible Man is a rollicking farce about havoc in a village whose norm is invaded by the visible invisible, as the Invisible Man swings from pitiable unseen, like that outcast, the tramp he meets, to corrupted Unseen with the status of an invisible god using the tramp as his pawn, from which state he promotes himself to invisible banker – people watching fistfuls of stolen money 'travelling without visible agency' along the roads : 'money . . . quietly and dexterously making off' from shops and inns 'in handfuls'. Power, greed and megalomania bloat and corrupt him and he starts to threaten the village, the town, the whole land, with the murderousness he can now get away with undetected, and with 'a reign of terror' – 'all who disobey his orders he must kill.' It's a book about seeing what we're blind to, a book full of masks, hubris, and 'the dream of a terrorised world'. Yet it's also a comedy, of selfishness and small-mindedness.

As a writer, Wells routs the romantic. His people are always ordinary people; his adventure books are notable precisely for their lack of heroes and conventional heroism; his people are too human and complex for it. His works are psychologically interesting and complex, always equivocating, often dealing with the split states we all deal with every day – sometimes on a larger symbolic level like the time traveller in The Time Machine caught between the childlike innocent upperworld beings and the ugly cannibalistic lowerworld monster beings whose Freudian dichotomy you might say inhabits us all. He writes with down-to-earthness about unearthly matters: 'In a little while it seemed to me as if I had always been alone on the moon.' He often seems to be talking, via the machines of his stories, about the self in trauma – 'strange mind of man!' the narrator in The War of the Worlds says, 'that with our species upon the edge of extermination or appalling degradation' can sit and play cards regardless of the Martians wandering about cherry-picking other humans to eat and flame-throwing them to death.

The War of the Worlds opens with a paragraph in which there's a bouleversing of the 'infinite complacency' of the ruling elite countries and the Empire. Its Martians, in their ghastly spindly tripods, with their 'leisurely parody of a human stride', are a leisurely parody of so-called human achievement. Seeing those great poisonous deadly Delphic-tripod Martian machines stalking the countryside, the narrator says, 'Can you imagine a milking-stool tilted and bowled violently along the ground?' It signals the end of the pastoral and simultaneously rings all the way back to Defoe's Journal of the Plague Years, all the formative fictive truth-tellers who knew that a combination of fiction and truth engendered the form of the novel. It signals an end to the English traditional novel too – and though Woolf and Joyce were to shape this end more formally viscerally, it permits, gives birth to, a shattering of traditions a quarter of a century before the modernists start to shake the structures for themselves. Its last page contains a moment that's Eliotic and written decades before The Waste Land:

I go to London and see the busy multitudes in Fleet Street and the Strand, and it comes across my mind that they are but the ghosts of the past, haunting the streets that I have seen silent and wretched, going to and fro, phantasms in a dead city.

Wells loved the persuasions of a real map – Doctor Moreau's fantasy island of mutant vivisected creatures is kept believable partly by its references to Gower Street and Tottenham Court Road, and you can trace with your finger on the real London map the route the Invisible Man takes through it, because Wells wanted books to relate to reality, and vice versa, and he knows how to layer reality and impossibility into a gift of palimpsest vision, all the more so for the familiarity.

> For the writer of fantastic stories to help the reader to play the game properly, he must help him in every possible unobtrusive way to *domesticate* the impossible hypothesis. He must trick him into an unwary concession to get some plausible assumption and get on with his story while the illusion holds.

Such 'tricks' a writer like Woolf would inevitably find 'rather thin spread – bread comes through', and some of his stories are machines every bit as self-consciously clunky as the time traveller's time machine, half-bicycle, half-fairground ride. But Woolf does him a disservice in her famous essay Character in Fiction when she imagines how, given the task of inventing an everyday character, a poorly dressed middle-aged woman on a train, he'd ignore her altogether and 'instantly project upon the window-pane a vision of a better, breezier, jollier, happier, more adventurous and gallant world . . . where miraculous barges bring tropical fruit to Camberwell by eight o'clock in the morning; where there are public nurseries, fountains, and libraries, dining-rooms, drawing-rooms, and marriages; where every citizen is generous and candid, manly and magnificent, and rather like Mr Wells himself'. Has she forgotten those earlier novels, or overlooked the darkness in his socio-realism? I can't believe here that Woolf's read anything but his worst, least-defining works, or hasn't been blinded by the social and political presence of the public man himself; it seems to me that he is existentialist through and through. She accuses him, elsewhere, of too much clay in the mix, 'the great clod of clay that has got itself mixed up with the purity of his inspiration'. I think it's the clod of clay that *is* his inspiration, the clod that makes us equivocating, unheroic, unpoetic, likely, earthy and earthly.

He never loses sight of what it means to be human, though always with a deep pessimism, probably an influence of his early days, when he studied biology under T. H. Huxley, otherwise known as Darwin's Bulldog. 'I tell you,' a character says to Kipps in the novel called Kipps, 'we're in a blessed drainpipe, and we've got to crawl along it till we die.' Wells knew by experience 'the great stupid machine' of industrial trade, 'a vast irresistible force' that drained the life-blood out of the humans that served it. There *was* no God to make these humans out of clay. There was only what we make of the world that made us, and what we make of and for other people. Wells's books are full of people who'll happily eat other people and terrorize other people, people capable of the kind of cynicism the man in The First Men in the Moon shows when he looks at the capsule his rather eccentric neighbour has constructed out of a new material he's invented that's capable of space travel, and looks at the moon way up there in the sky, and thinks about how much money he can make from a material that tough:

> My first natural impulse was to apply this principle to guns and ironclads and all the material and methods of war . . . my redemption as a business man . . . a parent company and daughter companies, applications to right of us, applications to left, rings and trusts, privileges, and concessions spreading and spreading, until one vast, stupendous . . . company ran and ruled the world.

He's never just one thing, though, Wells; his pessimism is cheery, useful, its satire is a kind of weapon, a shield, a cutting remark back at what time, history and humans might bring each other. He's a socialist, as well as an aesthetic pessimist. 'I fluctuate, I admit, between at the best a cautious and qualified optimism and my persuasion of swiftly advancing, irretrievable disaster,' he said. His first novel, The Time Machine, is unbelievably bleak in its projection of the future, one of 'horror . . . great darkness', a slime and crab evolution, evolution going backwards, and its time traveller comes back from that future, where humans will eat each other, rather alarmingly calling for meat himself – as if he's learned nothing.

And at the end of Wells's own time-travelling? Is there an education to be had, in our history, that *can* outrun catastrophe?

H. G. Wells wrote several classic, visionary novels about the very worst consequences a past and a present can have on a future – and a great deal of what he wrote, though it takes fantasy form, has come to pass, with stunning corollaries with his own time, the time after him, with our own time, and presumably with the as-yet-unwritten time ahead of us too.

So. What did the socialist visionary, the great, very human, far-seeing man, whose literary rise and circulation in the world had made him exceptionally powerful and exceptionally thoughtful about the workings of power, the man who'd been invited to meet and advise both Roosevelt and Stalin, who'd worked on ways, in his latter years, to 'release a new form of power in the world', a power 'without tyranny', one 'to hold men's minds together in something like a common interpretation of reality' and a real 'unification of our race' and to work for 'our collective life' –

What could such a profoundly prophetic writer do, who not only knew but drew for us the thin line between fantasy and reality, possibility and impossibility, and who so convincingly, prophetically and repeatedly envisioned the worst possible things that the world, the universe and the human beings in it can do to each other?

This.

He helped form and sustain PEN, where an internationality of writers would come together and think the world, and fight for and protect each other's freedom to write and freedom to read.

He helped form and sustain the National Council for Civil Liberties, we know it now as Liberty, to monitor and fight for the civil liberties that human beings need and that weak or bullying governments who want all the power will always want to mess with.

Above all, what we needed to do, Wells believed, was make and ratify as law an international declaration of human rights. In his final years of life, Wells was a core contributor to the Sankey Declaration of the Rights of Man, in fact he was the most active member of its committee, the main drafter of its clauses of fundamental human rights, his versions of which were closely followed in the eventual drafting of the wording for the 1948 UN Declaration of Human Rights, shortly after Wells's own death in 1946.

Our own Human Rights Act finally passed into law as late as 1998, incorporating into British law for the first time the European Convention on Human Rights, protecting human rights all across Europe and ratified by forty-seven member states (in fact, the UK was one of the first countries to ratify it in 1951, supported, especially by Churchill, as a protection against the possible return of fascism). The current government of the UK, now a hundred days old, announced as soon as it took office that it fully intends to scrap the Human Rights Act, that's the word they always use, though God help me I find it an obscenity, those words scrap and human and rights together in any sentence. That's what I call evolution going backwards.

But it's okay – *There is invisible support all around you*. Whether Fortuna the online goddess is right or not, Wells was wise enough to call for a much more visible form of support after a lifetime of seeing the dark of the future and the fragility of the light in people's eyes. He had known what it meant, since his first years as a writer, to be human and thought of as somewhat alien. And since 1896, when he was a young man writing The Island of Doctor Moreau, a book all about the beast in the human, he'd been interested in how at the mercy of the random or self-serving lawmakers we are. He was in his seventies when he wrote The Rights of Man, 'using "man" of course,' as he said, 'to cover every individual male or female, child or adult, of the species'.

Knowing too well in 1940 how little the League of Nations had been able to 'banish armed conflict from the world', he called, in The Rights of Man, for 'a profound reconstruction of the methods of human living'. What are we fighting for? was his question. His answer: 'a code of fundamental human rights which shall be made easily accessible to everyone'.

His initial draft included most of the things you can still find in our current Human Rights Act, and is especially, and interestingly presciently, strong on rights to privacy and dismissal of secrecy. 'All registration and records about citizens shall be open to their personal and private inspection. There shall be no secret dossiers in any administrative department.'

Here are the other suggested rights, in short. Right to nourishment, housing, health care and mental care :

right to education : right to have home and private property protected : right to work and earn and be free from slavery : right to move freely about the world : right to public trial and to detention for a short fixed time only : freedom from torture and degrading or inhuman treatment : right not to be force-fed nor stopped from hunger strike if you so choose : and right to finite imprisonment terms.

He spends the book tinkering with the precise word-ings of these suggested rights, to get it right, because on the one hand, 'in its thickets', as he puts it, 'govern-mental activities can interweave with, and at last become indistinguishable from organized crime'. On the other hand, 'the primary objective of every sane social order is to banish fear . . . from human life'.

Here's the invisible Wells, writing seventy-five years ago:

The enormous change in human conditions to which nearly all our present stresses are due, the abolition of distance and the stupendous increase in power, have flung together the population of the world so that a new way of living has become imperative . . . The elaboration of methods and material has necessitated a vast development and refinement of espionage, and in addition the increasing difficulty of understanding what the warfare is really about has produced new submersive and demoralizing activities of rumour-spreading, propaganda and the like, that complicate and lose contact at last with any rational objective . . .

The uprooting of millions of people who are driven into exile among strangers, who are forced to seek new homes, produces a peculiar exacerbation of the mental strain. Never have there been such crowds of migrating, depressing people. They talk languages we do not understand . . . They stimulate xenophobia without intention . . . Their necessary discordance with the new populations they invade releases and intensifies the natural distrust and hostility of man for man – which it is the aim of all moral and social training to eliminate . . .

For the restoration and modernization of human civilization, this exaggerated outlawing of the fellow citizen whom we see fit to suspect as a traitor or revolutionary and also of the stranger within our gates, has to be restrained and brought back within the scheme of human rights.

Given how familiar all this sounds, it's certainly interesting that our own Human Rights Act is right now under attack. You can read it, and find out about the threat to it, online. Look up Liberty, who've got a strong Save Our Human Rights Act campaign that needs us all right now. Look up PEN. Look up Amnesty International.

The government keeps calling it Labour's Human Rights Act. It's not. It was a cross-party formation, and it's ours, it belongs to all of us. They want to replace it with a British bill of rights – as if all nationalities are equal, but some are more equal than others. Wells would have dismissed outright the argument for a British bill of rights in the interest of 'the claims of the common man', claims 'against any government that seeks to defeat, exploit or betray' those common claims.

Back in 1940 he is facing his own 'incalculable government', and wants one that will 'declare for these rights unequivocally – or get out'. To paraphrase him slightly: an act of gross cruelty or injustice that occurs anywhere, wherever it happens, is just as much a British person's concern, a Scottish person's concern, an English person's, an Irish person's, a Welsh person's, a [fill in the blank with a nationality of your choice] person's concern. He knew, as Saramago puts it in his great novel Seeing: 'rights aren't abstractions, they continue to exist even when they're not respected'.

'There is no source of law,' Wells says, 'but the whole people, and since life flows on constantly to new citizens, no generation of the people can in whole or in part surrender or delegate the legislative power inherent in mankind.' Ah, he was an optimist after all. Ah, there *is* a heroic in his very human denial of heroes and heroism. There is wildness and revolution in his work, and above all an eye to a future that looks from here to be invisible, but that's always just a stone's-throw away.

Borges thought Wells's books, especially the early fantastic classics, would last for ever, 'be incorporated, like the fables . . . into the general memory of the species and even transcend . . . the extinction of the language in which they were written'. Well, that's a form of very ultimate success. Wells was a bit more short-term about it: 'The only true measure of success is the ratio between what we might have done and what we might have been on the one hand, and the thing we have made and the things we have made of ourselves, on the other.'

So. You, me, now, here we are. Here it all is. Here it comes. It's on our watch. (To observe the progress of, maintain an interest in. To have in one's care, to look after, to guard, to tend. From the Old English: to wake.) What'll we stand for? A couple of minutes an hour? Or what we call the future?

And on the other hand, what won't we stand for?

Preface

1

In this compact booklet, it is proposed to tell the story of a Manifesto which its Authors believe could be made a very useful and important document at the present time. It is a piece of associated writing of which the present writer is to be regarded as the editor and secretary rather than the author, and it first took shape in the form of two letters to the London *Times*. Therein we have the first statement of an idea that has developed in substance and importance with the impact of other experienced and critical minds. We believe that to many readers this gradual crystallization step by step of a definite politico-social creed may prove much more stimulating and interesting than the mere formal statement of creed. To them this book is dedicated.

The original *Times* letter ran as follows:

'WAR AIMS

'THE NEED FOR LIMITLESS CANDOUR

'To the Editor,
'*The Times*.
'SIR,

'I have been following the correspondence upon War Aims in your columns with considerable attention. In many respects it recalls the War Aims Controversy of 1917–18 when the Crewe House organization did its unsuccessful best to extract from the Foreign Office a precise statement of what the country was fighting for (see Sir Campbell Stuart's *Secrets of Crewe House*). No such statement was ever produced and the Great War came to a ragged end in mutual accusations of broken promises and double crossing.

'Even then there was a world-wide feeling that a great revolution in human affairs was imminent; the phrase "a war to end war" expressed that widely diffused feeling, and surely there could be no profounder break with human tradition and existing forms of government, than that. But that revolution did not realize itself. The League of Nations, we can all admit now, was a poor and ineffective outcome of that revolutionary proposal to banish armed conflict from the world and inaugurate a new life for mankind. It was too conservative of existing things, half-hearted, diplomatic. And since, as more and more of us are beginning to realize now, there can be no more peace or safety on earth without a profound reconstruction of the methods of human living, the Great War did not so much come to an end as smoulder through two decades, the fatuous 'twenties and the frightened 'thirties, to flare up again now. Now at a level of greater tension, increased violence and destructiveness and more universal suffering, we are back to something very like 1914 and the decisive question before our species is whether this time it will set its face resolutely towards that drastic remoulding of ideas and relationships, that world revolution, which it has shirked for a quarter of a century.

'If that revolution is to be brought off successfully and give a renewed lease to human happiness and effort, it is to be brought off only by the fullest, most ruthless discussion of every aspect and possibility of the present situation. Nobody and no group of people knows enough for this immense reorganization, and unless we can have a full and fearless public intercourse of minds open to all the world, our present enemies included, we shall never be able to establish a guiding system of ideas upon which a new world order can rest.

'We have before us as an object lesson the great

experiment of Russia. Whatever anyone may think of the outcome of the socialist movement which found its main embodiment in communism after 1848, there can be little dispute now of the fundamental nobility of that conception of a world-wide international system of social justice, a world peace, from which the incentive of private profit was to be eliminated. But from the beginning this movement encountered repression. It could not say what it had to say plainly and fearlessly. It was universalism with an involuntary hole-and-corner flavour.

'The result of suppressing the full, free discussion of revolutionary proposals, even of the extremest revolutionary proposals, is to force them underground. This sort of thing does not save an outworn and decaying regime but it drives the critics who are discussing a new order to conspiratorial methods, to terroristic secrecy, to unventilated dogmatism. The revolution, when at last it arrived in Russia, was in the hands of men trained in underground methods, and the Soviet regime, practically inexpert, with everything to learn, shut down on free discussion and free mutual criticism with the West, and degenerated into the masked incalculable personal rule of to-day. That was revolution in the dark. Cannot our Western world, in its quite inevitable march towards a world collectivism, face its changes in the light, in an atmosphere of extreme candour and mutual toleration? The thing I am most terrified by to-day is the manifest threat of a new weak put-off of our aspirations for a new world, by some repetition of the Geneva simulacrum. Last time it was the League of Nations; this time the magic word to do the trick is Federation. A real League of Nations might have turned the world into a new course in 1918–19; a real Federation of Mankind might do as much to-morrow. But if it is to be a real, effective federation of mankind, a genuine attempt to realize that age of world-wide plenty and safety that we have every reason to suppose attainable, then we have to discuss simply and sincerely and work out plans for the polite mediatization of monarchies, the competent socialization of the natural resources and staple industries of the world, the revision and extension of our universities and other knowledge organizations and the establishment of a world-wide rising level of common education. The war, under the auspices of A.R.P., is darkening everything. Are we to have as much light as that in the streets of the world? If not; if we are to go on with this present regime of vague insincerities, mutual distrust and sabotage, I for one can see no hope for mankind. More of this sort of thing and worse to the end.

'Yours faithfully,

'H. G. WELLS.'

After some correspondence a second letter appeared in *The Times* to this effect:

'To The Editor
'*The Times*.

'Sir,

'You recently did me the honour of printing a letter upon the possibility of discussing the outcome of this war while it is still going on, in which I stressed the need for free and outspoken discussion. This letter produced a considerable response and it has been reprinted extensively in America and elsewhere. I have been favoured by the views and comments of a number of very able people. With your permission I will give certain things that have become much clearer in this discussion as it has proceeded. The first is the extensive demand for a statement of "War Aims" on the part of young and old, who want to know more precisely what we are fighting for, and the second is the practical impossibility of making any statement in terms of boundaries, federations and political readjustments at the present time. This demand and this difficulty are not so mutually contradictory as they seem at first. There is a way of answering the demand in a very satisfactory manner without any of the entanglements involved in map-drawing, constitution-mongering, schemes for pledges, guarantees, sanctions and the like, and it is a method which is entirely in the best traditions of the Atlantic Parliamentary peoples; the method of a declaration of rights. At various crises in the history of our communities, beginning with Magna Carta and going through various Bills of Rights, Declarations of the Rights of Man and so forth, it has been our custom to produce a specific declaration of the broad principles on which our public and social life is based, and to abide by that as our fundamental law. The present time seems peculiarly suitable for such a restatement of the spirit in which we face life in general and the present combat in particular. It would answer the first question completely; it would furnish a criterion for our subsequent treaties and behaviour.

'In conjunction with a few friends I have drafted a trial statement of the rights of man brought up to date. I think that this statement may serve to put the War Aims discussion upon a new and more hopeful footing. It really involves nothing that is not actually observed or tacitly accepted by a great majority of reasonable men in the democratic states of to-day, it defines the spirit in which the mass of our people are more or less consciously fighting, and it is calculated to appeal very forcibly to every responsive spirit under the yoke of the obscurantist and totalitarian tyrannies with which we are in conflict.

'Declaration of Rights

'Since a man comes into this world through no fault of his own, since he is a joint inheritor of the accumulations of the past, and since those accumulations are more than sufficient to satisfy the claims that are here made on his behalf, it follows:

'(1) That every man without distinction of race or colour is entitled to nourishment, housing, covering, medical care and attention sufficient to realize his full possibilities of physical and mental development and to keep him in a state of health from his birth to death.

'(2) That he is entitled to sufficient education to make him a useful and interested citizen, that he should have easy access to information upon all matters of common knowledge throughout his life and enjoy the utmost freedom of discussion.

'(3) That he and his personal property lawfully acquired are entitled to police and legal protection from private violence, deprivation, compulsion and intimidation.

'(4) That although he is subject to the free criticism

of his fellows, he shall have adequate protection from any lying or misrepresentation that may distress or injure him. All registration and records about citizens shall be open to their personal and private inspection. There shall be no secret dossiers in any administrative department. All dossiers shall be accessible to the man concerned and subject to verification and correction at his challenge. A dossier is merely a memorandum; it cannot be used as evidence without proper confirmation.

'(5) That he may engage freely in any lawful occupation, earning such pay as the need for his work and the increment it makes to the common welfare may justify. That he is entitled to demand employment and to a free choice when there is any variety of employment open to him. He may suggest employment for himself and have his claim publicly considered.

'(6) That he may move freely about the world at his own expense. That his private house or apartment or reasonably limited garden enclosure is his castle, which may be entered only with his consent, but that he shall have the right to roam over any kind of country, moorland, mountain, farm, great garden or what not, where his presence will not be destructive of its special use nor dangerous to himself nor seriously inconvenient to his fellow-citizens.

'(7) That he shall have the right to buy or sell without any discriminatory restrictions anything which may be lawfully bought or sold, in such quantities and with such reservations as are compatible with the common welfare.

'(8) That a man unless he is duly certified as mentally deficient shall not be imprisoned for a longer period than three weeks without being charged with a definite offence against the law, nor for more than three months without a public trial. At the end of the latter period, if he has not been tried and sentenced by due process of law, he shall be released.

'(9) That no man shall be subjected to any sort of mutilation or sterilization except with his own deliberate consent, freely given, nor to bodily assault, except in restraint of his own violence, nor to torture, beating or any other bodily punishment; he shall not be subjected to imprisonment with such an excess of silence, noise, light or darkness as to cause mental suffering, or to imprisonment in infected, verminous or otherwise insanitary quarters, or be put into the company of verminous or infectious people. He shall not be forcibly fed nor prevented from starving himself if he so desire. He shall not be forced to take drugs nor shall they be administered to him without his knowledge. That the extreme punishments to which he may be subjected are rigorous imprisonment for a term of not longer than fifteen years or death.

'(10) That the provisions and principles embodied in this Declaration shall be more fully defined in a legal code which shall be made easily accessible to everyone. This Declaration shall not be qualified nor departed from upon any pretext whatever. It incorporates all previous declarations of human right. Henceforth it is the fundamental law for mankind throughout the world.'

2

Simultaneously the idea was put before a number of publicists and writers for their criticism and co-operation, and various organizations subjected it to a very helpful criticism. A preamble, differing from the *Times* opening, approaching the matter from a different angle, was distributed widely with copies of the draft. This preamble said:

'Preamble

'The destruction of confidence is one of the less clearly recognized evils of the present phase of world-disintegration.

'In the past there have been periods when whole communities, or at least large classes within communities, have gone about their business with a general honesty, directness and sense of personal honour. They have taken a keen pride in the quality of their output. They have lived through life on tolerable and tolerant terms with their neighbours. The laws they observed have varied in different countries and periods, but their general nature was to make an orderly law-abiding life possible and natural. They had been taught and they believed, and they had every reason to believe: "This (that or the other thing) is right. Do right and nothing, except by some strange exceptional misfortune, can touch you. Do right and nothing will rob you or frustrate you. The Law guarantees you that."

'Nowhere in the world now is there very much of that feeling left, and as it disappears, the behaviour of people degenerates towards a panic scramble, towards cheating, over-reaching, gang organization, precautionary hoarding, concealment and all the meanness and anti-social feeling which is the natural outcome of insecurity.

'Faced with what now amounts to something like a moral stampede, on the part of governments quite as much as individuals, more and more sane men will realize the urgency for a restoration of confidence. The more socialization proceeds and the more directive authority is concentrated, the more necessary is an efficient protection of individuals from the impatience of well-meaning or narrow-minded or ruthless or dishonest officials and indeed from all the possible abuses of advantage that are inevitable under such circumstances to our still childishly wicked breed.

'In the past the Atlantic world has been particularly successful in expedients for meeting this aspect of human nature. Our characteristic and traditional method may be called the method of the fundamental declaration. Our Western peoples, by a happy instinct, have produced statements of right, from Magna Carta onwards, to provide a structural defence between the citizen and the necessary growth of central authority.

'And plainly the successful organization of the more universal and penetrating collectivism that is now being forced upon us all, will be frustrated in its most vital aspect unless its organization is accompanied by the preservative of a new declaration of the rights of man, that must because of the increasing complexity of the new social structure be more generous, detailed and explicit than any of its predecessors. Such a Declaration must become the *common fundamental law* of all communities and collectivities assembled under the World Pax. It should be interwoven with the declared war aims of the combatant powers now; it should become the primary fact in any settlement; it should be put before the now combatant states for their approval, their embarrassed silence or their rejection.

'In order to be as clear as possible about this, let me submit a draft for your consideration of this proposed declaration of the rights of man – using "man" of course to cover every individual male or female, child or adult, of the species. I have endeavoured to bring in everything that is essential and to omit whatever secondary issues can be easily deduced from its general statements. It is a draft for your consideration. Points may have been overlooked, and it may contain repetitions and superfluous statements.'

And here followed the original draft already given in the second *Times* letter.

3

The reception of the draft thus published and circulated was very favourable. It was realized that it was a timely and far-reaching suggestion, and most of the adverse comment seemed not so much to meet it as slide away from it upon imaginary issues raised by reading 'between the lines'. The next step seemed to be to revise it thoroughly, disposing of or incorporating every proposed amendment that seemed to be relevant. If the Declaration was worth making at all, it was worth going over thoroughly to make it as good as possible.

This little booklet is a summary of that revision, so that the reader can follow and appreciate the motives for every step in its development.

We discuss the Declaration clause by clause with the underlying justifications for its phrasing and amendment. It is emphasized that such a Declaration is in no way a novel thing in the political life of Western Europe and America, and that at the present time it is absolutely necessary for the consolidation, implementing and control of the revolutionary impulses that are astir all over the world. For manifestly the world is either in revolution or in collapse. The choice is not between accepting revolution and keeping on as we are, but between accepting revolution or destroying it and ourselves.

The book opens upon a journalistic and contemporary note, it prefaces itself for the third time; we hammer it in. Almost everything of significance is repeated several times, but almost always with a new intensification. The record had to take that form. It is a work that accumulates as it proceeds, and it seeks to evoke a continual collaboration in the reader.

I

Imperative Need for a Declaration

The whole world is asking for the War Aims of the Allied Powers, and we British and our Allies are damping enthusiasm at home and throughout the Empire and losing the moral support of America and the neutral countries generally, by the failure of our Governments to make any lucid statement of their war intentions.

It is stupid to say 'Wait until the war is won.' Any sensible man who fights, fights to win; that goes without saying. And he has an Aim. A man who fights to win without any Aim before him, can find a readier relief for his pugnacity than the laborious restraints, discomforts and uncertainties of modern warfare. Most modern men have no set craving for fighting, and they are asking now with an increasing querulousness why their private lives are being disorganized and why they are being dragged, pushed, exhorted, compelled into a vast war effort, with no assurance whatever that any worth-while results at all, are to come out of it.

And our Government, the people who are ordering and pushing us about – and doing it in an obviously very incompetent way – makes no statement that is in any way reassuring and stimulating. Great Britain pretends to be a 'democracy', that is to say a rule of, by and for the people, etc., etc. Consequently *our* Government is assumed to be acting under *our* instructions. Yet it gives no sign of what it imagines these instructions to be. It will not say what it imagines it is up to. So far as we are able to judge, it does not know. But it will not admit it does not know. This inefficient Government of ours has been clutching hysterically to strangle liberty of discussion and protest. (Thank Heaven for Mr Dingle Foot!) Our individual liberties are being threatened by emergency legislation. Our representatives, our ministries and servants are out of hand.

Let me say while it is still sayable that we have no particular confidence in the Prime Minister; he has never given evidence of marked ability of any sort; his record as a business man is anything but brilliant; he was one of Mr Lloyd George's failures during the last war; he impresses us as having the peevish secretiveness of a man who cannot stand criticism; his preference for mediocrities in office and his manifest jealousy of special gifts and abilities may quite conceivably lose us this war – with everything in our favour – and few of us feel safe with him. Nor do we feel safe with our Foreign Office. For all we know the war is already being sold by secret treaty, behind our backs. That happened during the last war. Yet we are unable to get any alternative government. It seems impossible to persuade people that there can be worse things than a change of Government during war time, and that Mr Chamberlain is one of them. Consequently the desire to see him and his Government pinned to some clear statement of what it is all about, is growing urgent and more general. We want War Aims now.

We are not fighting the Germans. Everyone agrees to that. Our Government most of all. We are fighting Hitler and the Nazis. We want to *free* the Germans. And so we may point out how very similar is the predicament of these friends of ours, these Germans, whom we are fighting to liberate, to our own. They too find themselves marched off to war and undergoing, I am told, far greater privations and even more tiresome regulations than our own. They too, we are told, have a considerable distrust of their leaders. They too want to know what it is all about. But obviously they can no more get rid of Hitler than we can get rid of Mr Chamberlain, and Hitler anyhow has at least the prestige of being in his rough way a successful man. His Propaganda Minister tells these Germans we are so acutely anxious to free, quite awful stories of what will happen to them if they don't fight. It is a rather clever propaganda and it quotes every foolish threat against Germany to keep them at the desperate pitch. They are going to be liberated from the Nazi yoke, our leaflets tell them, and instead of being simply grateful about it and sabotaging Herr Hitler, they ask: 'What then?'

'What then?' they ask. 'What then?' And that is where Herr Goebbels finds his opportunity.

India too is saying: 'Yes, we will support you in this war, *but* someday it will end; probably in a sort of muddling-through you will win it, and then what?'

And while we British, thus challenged, stand embarrassed behind our ambiguous government, the hostile propaganda profits by that silence. All sorts of indiscreet, unwise and possibly treacherous utterances are made. Mr Duff Cooper, landing at New York, cools his mind by blowing off about a forthcoming revolt of the German Army and a return to monarchy in Germany, a Holy Roman Empire, I suppose, leading that new Crusade of which the Pope has been talking recently against anti-God Russia. But quite a lot of radical people in the world, in spite of the folly, stupidity and brutality of the Stalin–Molotov attack on Finland, are averse from this idea of a religious war against Socialism and Atheism. Nor is a rally of mankind under the banner of the Vatican a stimulating outlook for Protestant and any Social Democratic Germans who survive! An obscure periodical in Toulouse unfolds a project for cutting up our beloved Germans when we have liberated them from Nazi oppression (and extracted proper indemnities) into a number of small, entirely disarmed servile states. This stuff goes into Germany at once. 'This,' says the German radio, 'is what they mean to do with you! This is what those British leaflets did not tell you! You see, you must fight. It will be *Little Man what now?* all over again and worse if you don't.'

We common British intend nothing of the sort. In a dim, deep, instinctive way our people are setting about this war, reluctantly, seriously and resolutely. We want to bring Nazi aggression to a standstill and admitted defeat. And we have no clear ideas at all about what is to happen to Germany afterwards. We do not believe it is practicable to cut up Germany, and we have not the remotest idea of fighting in this religious war between the Vatican and Russia. We know that we have been forced and misled into a position when we are bound to go on fighting. We are fighting against lawless violence; that is to say, we are fighting that 'war to end war' which began on August 4th, 1914. We were cheated in 1918, and put off with the Geneva League of the Victorious Powers for twenty years, and we have muddled along to this. And this time we are clearer about it and we want our Government to implement our will. We are fighting to abolish violence, we, the common people of Britain and France, because we find it impossible to live the lives we want to live, in a belligerent world. We want to end war for ever. That in the broadest terms is our War Aim.

We want to have no more mistakes about it this time. We do not want another patched-up politicians' muddle. And so, taught by the frustrations of the League of Nations period, we are setting ourselves to discover how we realize that essential aim. Certain necessities are becoming very clear again to more and more of us. And the first of these is to do again what it has been the practice of the Parliamentary peoples to do whenever they come to a revolutionary turning-point of their histories, which is to make a declaration of the fundamental principles upon which the new phase is to be organized. This was done to check the encroachments of the Crown in Magna Carta. The particular Petition of Right made in 1628 repeated this expedient. It was done again in the Declaration of Right and the Bill of Rights which ended the 'Leviathan' and the Divine Right of Kings. Magna Carta and the Bill of Rights are an integral part of American law. The American Declaration of Independence was another such statement of a people's will, and the French Declaration of the Rights of Man derived its inspiration directly from that document.

Now that we are at another great turning-point of human history, we need another fundamental assertion of the supremacy of the claims of the common man against any privilege, pre-emption or government whatever. We want to assert our claims against any government that seeks to defeat, exploit or betray them. We need a new Declaration of Rights, and one of such a nature that it will involve an ultimate repudiation of violence and warfare from end to end of the earth.

What should be the clauses of such a Declaration to-day? All the conditions of human life have been profoundly altered during the last two centuries, and it will have to differ from its predecessors in many particulars. New occasions have arisen and old grievances ceased to distress us. I propose now to go over the draft for such a Declaration, as it has been amended, clause by clause. I feel that when we have established the form of that fundamental law, then and then only will it be possible to take up the detached problems of the War Aims that we encounter on our way towards our fundamental aim, the riddle of conflicting powers, boundaries, nations, races, minorities, with some assurance that they will fall into a reasonable and hopeful outlook for a new World Order.

We want to draw up a document and demand of Mr Chamberlain and his friends abroad and at home: 'Is this what we are fighting for? And if not then please tell us what you imagine we *are* fighting for?

'Or better, perhaps, get out.'

II

Security from Violence

In its original form the draft Declaration of Rights began with a preamble and proceeded in an orderly fashion from a statement of primary physical needs up to the provision of a legal world code. That was how it had come off my mind. But I found that most of the people and the younger men in particular who were going to do the fighting, with whom I discussed the declaration, were not prepared to receive it in quite the same order. They wanted to have it put another way round.

They were moved principally by two things. Firstly, they felt the need of fighting again to 'put down violence' in the world, to go on with the war to end war that had lost its way at Versailles, and secondly, they had been stirred profoundly by those outrages upon human dignity perpetrated by the Nazis. The second motive was perhaps the stronger. Many of them had been incredulous at first of the stories that came from concentration camps and refugees. When they realized reluctantly that such things could still be done in the heart of Europe, something like a lynching spirit was stirred up in them. The peace of the world receded into the background. 'These Nazis are *too* bad,' they said. The first thing they wanted in a Declaration of War Aims was a plain statement that such things must happen no more on earth.

This present warfare, the present recrudescence of the war to end war, is going to be much less of a sporting event, much grimmer and graver, than the 1914–18 struggle. Hardly anything sharpened the temper of the British troops then. They wouldn't even call the Germans 'Huns'; they called them 'Fritz' and 'Jerry', they treated their prisoners with a certain derisive affection, they respected the cry of 'Kamerad' right up to the end. I doubt if they are going to behave in quite the same way to the young Germany of Hitler, wearing its thick boots (that have stamped in the faces of Jewish women), its brown shirts, that recall the victims smothered in latrines and all the cloacal side of Hitlerism, its swastika – ignorantly stolen from the Semitic stone-age peoples; oafish and hysterically cruel. I guess that in face of this material the bayoneting this time will be done in a different spirit.

Grimmer and more serious warfare . . . Not only are

we likely to hear less of 'Fritz' and 'Jerry', but presently our own young men, whose lives are being crippled and disordered, will be found less amenable to the delights of being real 'Tommies', of hearing endless jokes about 'better 'oles' and 'Old Bill', of being entertained by troupes of third-rate comics, inundated with cigarettes and sent chocolate boxes and Christmas greetings from quite the most eminent people. 'We are here to clean up something,' they will say, 'something you gentlemen and ladies who are picnicking so bravely and merrily in evacuated and carefully camouflaged ministries "somewhere in England" failed to clear up after 1918. Will you get on with it this time so that we can come back to a real worth-while life? What exactly are you doing and what are you going to do, to stop this sort of brutality and foolery for ever? If we are assured you are doing something effective, we shall not grudge our sacrifices, but if we are to have all this pseudo-cheerful muck dug up, to remind us that this is just the dear old 1914–18 over again, well – the morale of this army may suffer.'

The least we can do, we elderly civilians who sit warm at home, protected by enormously exaggerated and madly expensive precautions from risks of the nature of one in ten thousand or less, is to work out what the country is fighting for and see whether this time we cannot get the goods delivered. We have to give our utmost to so co-ordinating and implementing the motives of the real fighters as to make them effective, and that is why we demand something more comprehensive, more lucid and more binding upon these gentlemen at Westminster and in the hide-outs than vague speeches and promises. The 'Tommies' were promised a land 'fit for heroes' last time. Let their sons bear that in mind. This time we want that sort of thing signed and in writing and defined and clear, we want to be sure that that promise has secured priority, before we get deafened and blinded by the fighting.

Now in this first draft which was made for that Declaration of Rights which is absolutely necessary, if the war is to reach any rational end – if, that is, we are to 'end war' – the repudiation of the brutality that has so greatly stirred us to combat, is put not as the first clause but as the ninth. In a subsequent chapter it will be shown that it does in fact depend for its effective realization upon preceding propositions of a more general character, but for our present purposes there is no reason why we should not pass upon that clause now. Here it is:

'(9) That no man shall be subjected to any sort of mutilation or sterilization except with his own deliberate consent, freely given, nor to bodily assault, except in restraint of his own violence, nor to torture, beating or any other bodily punishment; [he shall not be subjected to imprisonment with such an excess of silence, noise, light or darkness as to cause mental suffering, or to imprisonment in infected, verminous or otherwise insanitary quarters, or be put into the company of verminous or infectious people]. He shall not be forcibly fed nor prevented from starving himself if he so desire. He shall not be forced to take drugs not shall they be administered to him without his knowledge and consent. That the extreme punishments to which he may be subjected are rigorous imprisonment for a term of not longer than fifteen years or death.'

In this I have put certain phrases in brackets because they may be considered too detailed and redundant, but they are put in nevertheless, as so many provisions of Magna Carta were put in, to point a finger directly at some conspicuous contemporary abuse. And does the reader subscribe to that Clause 9? And if not, what has he against it? Shall we amend it, re-phrase it, bind ourselves to fight for it whenever necessary, or admit that the things we have cited in that clause are things that may be legally done by anyone in power, to us and our fellow creatures? The Nazis and the Communists think they are, and that is one main reason why we are under arms and at war.

The recently published White Paper makes it plain that *our Government has known for some time* that such things were going on, and yet that up to a late hour it was willing to make peace with those who are responsible for all these tortures and murders the White Paper now substantiates. I suppose if our Government had after all made that eleventh-hour peace, then all that is in the White Paper would have been hushed up. We should have sat down to our Christmas dinner thanking God for Mr Chamberlain and ignoring the concentration camps altogether. And this incalculable Government of ours is still quite capable of sitting down in some sort of Conference with the Nazis, the White Paper forgotten. We have no assurance that it will hold firmly to these common human rights for whose sake alone our people are willing to fight.

And so we want our Government to declare for these rights unequivocally — or get out.

III

Habeas Corpus

We are fighting this war for human freedom, for ending the perpetual tension of war, and a better way of living, or we are fighting for nothing worth fighting for. If we are to have a declaration of rights that will fully embody these aims and provide a sound basis for a new world order, much has to be added to that mere repudiation of manhandling and violence contained in the clause we have just discussed. We have next to frame a clause to ensure personal freedom.

In the draft declaration on which the present discussion is based, this was dealt with in Clause 8. Originally this clause provided merely that a man 'unless he is duly certified as mentally deficient', etc. This obviously excluded certified mental defectives, who were a different class altogether from lunatics, and it ignored certain glaring defects in the existing law affecting these unfortunates. The clause has since been amended in accordance with expert advice by the substitution of the words italicized. So amended it runs:

'(8) That a man *unless he is declared by a competent authority to be a danger to himself and to others through mental abnormality, a declaration which must be annually confirmed,* shall not be imprisoned for a longer period than six days without being charged with a definite offence against the law, nor for more than three months without a public trial. At the end of the latter period, if he has not been tried and sentenced by due process of law, he shall be released.'

The italicized amendment has evoked no hostile criticism at all. There has been a very enthusiastic endorsement of the proviso that the certification of the lunatic and mental defective shall be annually renewed. Hitherto the practice has been to say, 'Once a lunatic, always a lunatic,' and these words will introduce an element of hope into the lives of a peculiarly unhappy and often cruelly victimized class of human beings. I know of no practical objection to them, except in so far as the refusal to recognize that there are incurable lunatics may necessitate some modification in the phrasing of the current divorce law. But it is better to give our legislators a little trouble than to damn men for life.

Next it has been pointed out that even at present an arrest without a charge for even six days is against the theory, if not the practice, of English and American law. A man, it is said, unless caught red-handed should not be arrested without a warrant and that implies a charge made. Common sense and common practice mitigate this, and, for example, people are arrested for loitering under suspicious circumstances, they may be searched and so forth. I think it may be in the public interest in certain cases to give the police that *maximum* of six days in which to prepare and assemble evidence for a charge, but those who are better acquainted with the practices of the criminal law will know how far this extension of time might be abused. The rest of the clause as drafted is merely Magna Carta, adapted to the more speedy facilities of the present time.

But it is alleged by another group of critics that this Clause still leaves certain matters unsettled. There again I admit difficulties. They centre upon the idea of conscription. It is objected to the Declaration as a whole that it says much about rights and nothing about duties. It may be true that anyone who observes the rights of others to the full extent of the Declaration, has already undertaken very considerable obligations, but that does not dispose completely of this objection.

The valid criticism that still remains is to be found very competently set out by William James in a small but very important book, *The Moral Equivalent of War*.

He finds, and one must remember he was a very great and subtle psychologist, something very unsatisfactory and impracticable in the prospect of a world of peace and security in which everyone is to move about freely without any sense of ownership in the community, participation in the community or obligation to the community. The more collectivist we become – and continually we become more collectivist – the more the sense of proprietorship has to be transferred to the community as a whole. The community is something to which we look for the protection of our rights indeed, but it is also something we have to take care of and serve. And this is not to be attained by mere preachment and sentiment.

And so he suggests a universal conscription for one or two years of the formative period of life, somewhere between sixteen, let us say, and twenty-five, during which the young citizen, man or woman, will have to undertake some of that residue of unpleasing, irksome, dangerous or subordinate work that must still be done, whatever feats of mechanism or organization the future may have in store for us.

There are, for instance, the prisons, the lunatic asylums, the hospitals to be staffed, much of what is now called 'menial service' – there will still be handing round and washing up to do, even if there is no arbitrary 'ordering about' – many toilsome industrial operations, in mines, fisheries when the ships go out in all weathers, sanitary work. This sort of work is too abundant to be paid for highly and too unattractive for volunteers, and in any equalitarian state in which there are no longer subject races, it can only conceivably be done by *fags*, whose drudgery will presently be lifted in rotation from their shoulders.

No doubt the officers who will direct these services will be highly skilled and highly paid specialists, but the rank and file cannot be paid magnificently. Yet when it comes to a Declaration of Rights, it seems to me that this conscription has to be assumed as a possibility, rather than proclaimed as a duty, and so I suggest adding to that draft Clause this:

'Nor shall he be conscripted for military or any other service to which he has a conscientious objection.'

And having passed upon this Habeas Corpus Clause, we have now to take up the difficult question of laws and regulations. These world citizens for whose immunity and liberty Clause 8 and 9 have now provided, have to live in regulated relationships with each other. How are regulations and laws to be made in a democratic state so as to preserve the essential quality of democracy?

IV

Democratic Law

In a democratic state there are or should be laws of three very definite sorts and very different grades of importance. First of all there should be the *fundamental law* expanding and implementing the Declaration of Rights, and protecting the individual adequately from any abuse of administrative authority. The primary duty of the legal organization is to sustain these liberties.

But next comes a great body of law which has no relation to any moral issue whatever, and that is law to enforce conventions, *conventional law*. A typical convention is the rule of the road. There is no reason whatever in the nature of things why one should travel on the right side of the road rather than the left or *vice versa*, but traffic only becomes tolerable if a rule, a fundamentally irrational rule, is rigorously sustained with pains and penalties as a last resort. Another convention is the law against forgery. It is really a charming exercise, calling for the most delicate artistic gifts, to make an indistinguishable facsimile of the signature to a cheque, and still more so to imitate a monetary note, colour, texture and all, but since the whole system of commerce would break down if that sort of activity were permitted, it is an offence by convention and made crushingly punishable. These conventional laws belong to an entirely different order from the protection of fundamental rights. They need to be made with elaborate precautions against abuse or hardship.

A third type of law, *administrative law*, which may in some cases overlap the second, includes the enormous mass of legislation needed for the exploitation of the natural resources of the world in the common interest, and the prevention of waste and devastation by incoherent and short-sighted enterprise. This involves immense appropriations to technically competent authorities and their right not only to use and take, but to forbid and penalize the misuse of regions, minerals, forests, soils, waters. To restrain these delegated authorities from anti-social deterioration, and maintain their efficiency, it is plainly necessary to have the most outspoken and unrestrained criticism, discussion and publicity, and a definite power of calling these various administrative bodies to account.

Now here arises a problem in politico-legal

organization which cannot be solved except in a very general manner in such a discussion as this. Possibly the best method for dealing with an unsatisfactory administration of any type would be for a sufficient number of citizens to be able to demand a recall, an enquiry and if needed a reconstruction. But I will not develop that now. The point to make clear is that there are these three sorts of law: (*a*) the law of fundamental rights, (*b*) conventional law, to establish necessary conventions, and (*c*) administrative law, which becomes more and more important as human affairs advance towards collectivization, the enormous and various law of economic and social organization. So far as (*a*) goes, everyone should know the law; so far as (*b*) goes, everyone affected should know the conventions; but so far as (*c*) goes, the whole framework of laws is beyond any single person's knowing it and it needs to be clearly codified and continually revised and made easily accessible, so that anyone affected can easily inform himself upon the issue that concerns him.

Now in the light of this prelude we come to the tenth clause of that proposed declaration of rights, and it is evident how entirely inadequate was that first draft, and how necessary is an adaptive amendment. The minds of the framers of the original draft were manifestly so concentrated upon the Rights of the Individual (*a*) that they overlooked (*b*) and (*c*) entirely and so framed the clause as follows:

'(10) That the provisions and principles embodied in this Declaration shall be more fully defined in a legal code which shall be made easily accessible to everyone. This code shall not be qualified nor departed from upon any pretext whatever. It incorporates all previous Declarations of Human Right. Henceforth it is the fundamental law for mankind throughout the whole world.'

Now that can be amended by substituting in the first sentence for 'a legal code', 'a code of fundamental human rights'. But that still leaves it necessary to adjust law (*a*) to the powers needed by the conventional laws (*b*) and to the vastly complex requirements of law of type (*c*). And for that, something of this sort needs to be added.

'No treaty and no law affecting these primary rights shall be binding upon any man or province or administrative division of the community, that has not been made openly, by and with the active or tacit acquiescence of every adult citizen concerned, either given by a direct majority vote of the community affected or through the majority vote of his publicly elected representatives. In matters of collective behaviour it is by the majority decision that men must abide. No administration, under a pretext of urgency, convenience or the like, shall be entrusted with powers to create or further define offences or set up by-laws, which will in any way infringe the rights and liberties here asserted. All legislation must be public and definite. No secret treaties shall be binding on individuals, organizations or communities. No orders in council or the like which extend the application of a law shall be enforceable. There is no source of law but the whole people, and since life flows on constantly to new citizens, no generation of the people can in whole or in part surrender or delegate the legislative power inherent in mankind.'

So we can dot the i's and cross the t's of our original intention in Clause 10. As it stands thus underlined and corrected, I submit that it supplies a fairly adequate protection for our liberties. But the authors of the Declaration also drafted a fourth Clause, which may seem to some people an unnecessary amplification of Clause 10. This and the reasons for including it, we will now discuss.

V

The New Tyranny of the Dossier

In this draft Declaration of the Rights of Man we are discussing there is one other clause affecting personal liberty, Clause 4, that I now realize was misplaced. It should stand apart from the clauses providing for man's economic security. It should come immediately before Clause 8 dealing with the imprisonment and trial of the citizen. It aims at a vast jungle of private and administrative abuses in which nearly all our lives are now entangled, a jungle enormously fostered by warfare and the preparation for war. In its thickets governmental activities can interweave with, and at last become indistinguishable from organized crime.

The clause, amended by a word or so for the sake of greater explicitness, runs as follows:

'(4) That although a man is subject to the free criticism of his fellows, he shall have adequate protection from any lying or misrepresentation that may distress or injure him. All administrative registration and records about a man shall be open to his personal and private inspection. There shall be no secret dossiers in any administrative department. All dossiers shall be accessible to the man concerned and subject to verification and correction at his challenge. A dossier is merely a memorandum; it cannot be used as evidence without proper confirmation in open court.'

Very modestly but definitely this clause strikes at the forces and tendencies of our time that are rapidly diffusing a taint of insanity through the whole of human life. The enormous change in human conditions to which nearly all our present stresses are due, the abolition of distance and the stupendous increase in power, have flung together the population of the world so that a new way of living has become imperative, have not only made warfare more disorganizing and inconclusive but have also made its methods more socially penetrating and disconcerting. The elaboration of methods and material has necessitated a vast development and refinement of espionage, and in addition the increasing difficulty of understanding what the warfare is really about has produced new submersive and demoralizing activities of rumour-spreading, propaganda and the like, that complicate and lose contact at last with any rational objective. Any fool can tell a lie and too many fools like doing so. The sub-human malicious mischief of the young men a generation of Catholic education has produced in Southern Ireland, their senseless burning of letters in pillar boxes, their indiscriminate cutting of telephone wires and so forth, are a reminder to all of us how little mankind at large has risen above the level of an exceptionally spiteful ape, and how soon our kind can sink back again to that level. The White Paper on Nazi cruelties displays the same atavism in a heavier and filthier form. Warfare or sub-warfare, by releasing these baser impulses to opportunity, abolish that confidence and candour which alone make free, happy and generous living possible. The gallant, sure and open life has become impossible. In a brief third of a century it has become impossible.

The crowding together of mankind, the abolition of the non-combatant and the concentration of governments upon intensive militarism, to the relative neglect of education and training for the civilized life, have forced us all, whether we like it or not, into a state of insecurity, suspicion and precaution. Trust is evaporating. We live, from the dictator with his bodyguard of blackguards down to the humblest creature among us who may be robbed, raped, beaten up or enslaved, in the shadow of fear. It becomes more and more difficult to keep a mental balance and not to give way to storms of exasperation.

The uprooting of millions of people who are driven into exile among strangers, who are forced to seek new homes, produces a peculiar exacerbation of the mental strain. Never have there been such crowds of migrating, depressing people. They talk languages we do not understand, they have queer ways; they are not at home with us; they are often quite unaccountable. They stimulate xenophobia without intention; they cannot help doing it; and among them, finding a convenient cover among them, are the spy and the agent provocateur. It is no good pretending they are all innocent and harmless. They can be not only definitely malignant but without any malice they can be a serious economic disturbance. Their necessary discordance with the new populations they invade releases and intensifies the natural distrust and hostility of man for man – which it is the aim of all moral and social training to eliminate – to a dangerous degree.

One feels a certain justifiable wariness towards these outlanders, until one learns their forms of behaviour; until one realizes that they may do this but they can't do that, and so on. The ideally wise man may be able to retain such an observant balance, but normal people tend either to collapse into a sort of hysterical trustfulness on the one hand, or fall on the other side into exaggerated suspicion mania. The majority seem to fall on the side of mania, and under the stimulus of this mania there has accumulated a vast tangle of emergency legislation, regulations, barriers and restraints, out of all proportion to and often completely missing and distorting the needs of the situation. For the restoration and modernization of human civilization, this exaggerated outlawing of the fellow citizen whom we see fit to suspect as a traitor or revolutionary and also of the stranger within our gates, has to be restrained and brought back within the scheme of human rights.

Mingling with this factor of suspicion become frantic, there is also another unpleasant trait in our sinful make-up, and that is the craving to exercise power. Here is a great new opportunity for this craving. Enormous possibilities of insult, annoyance and frustration, enormous possibilities of inflicting needless anxiety, loss and misery, have been put in the hands of minor officials, and in many cases they are being exercised to the full, maliciously and needlessly, to the increasing distraction and embitterment of life. People find themselves now restricted in their movements, interned, expelled from countries, denied the common amenities of social life, on secret information, without any charge, without explanation, without the right to plead.

The net catches the foreigner first, but it spreads very readily to the native 'agitator', to the 'troublesome' employee, to the unjustly dismissed 'radical' among the workers. In the public services it takes the form of the 'secret and confidential' report. In such cases, indeed, the less a libel is published the greater the injury it may do. People jump at evil interpretations and the mischief is done. A man may be blighted for his lifetime by a misconception or a lie. He may never know clearly what entangles him. And so the framers of our Declaration worded a very explicit special clause against this lurking and increasing menace.

The primary objective of every sane social order is to banish fear – not necessarily to abolish danger, which by itself can stir men very pleasantly – but fear, from human life. Confidence and assurance are the essence of brotherliness; there is no ease in intercourse, no civilization, without them. Fear lies very near the surface of most animal life, but it need not do so in the life of man. It need not, but it does, and then it becomes a far more dreadful thing than mere animal fear. It does not pass. It goes on and on, and it gnaws.

Man, because of that restless excessive brain of his, complicates every issue in his life beyond comparison with the mental complexity of any other animal. He can go mad. A 'mad' bull is a bull in a rutting fury or a blind rage, it just 'sees red'; a 'mad' dog is an animal with a feverish infection; they are not really 'mad' in the elaborate, disordered way of human madness. But man can err and err fantastically, entanglement behind entanglement. He can go 'off the lines' of reason altogether. He can meet trouble more than half way and so break down under his worries and disappointments as to become 'certifiable'.

And that now seems to be happening to mankind as a whole. We are all in it. We are none of us as sane as our self-satisfied, limited, confident grandfathers. We are all fighting within ourselves for self-control. Unless we can struggle through the mounting perplexities of to-day, to a new world order of law and safety, unless we can keep our heads and our courage, so as to re-establish a candid life, our species will perish, mad, fighting and gibbering, a dwindling swarm of super-Nazis on a devastated earth.

P.S. – Certain practical considerations which necessitate a modification of this dossier clause are discussed at the end of Chapter XI.

VI
The Right to Subsistence

So far in this discussion of human rights we have dealt mainly with the assertion of persona freedom, because that is the aspect that come first to mind as a primary war issue now. When we oppose the 'democracies' to the 'dictatorships', that is what we have in mind. The clauses we have considered have been political and legal, and so far our Declaration has followed in the footsteps of its mighty predecessors from Magna Carta to the Declaration of the Rights of Man.

To make a sweeping generalization, the outline of the history of the Parliamentary peoples from the chaos of the early dark ages onward may be presented as a struggle for adjustment between a growing central power, typically represented in the past by the sovereign, and the free spirit of man. As human society recovered from that age of confusion, and as production, trade and population expanded, the need for larger unities of management became apparent. The King's law appeared, there was a consolidation of management, more and more regulation.

This Government law, this administrative law, I have already discussed, and distinguished sharply from the primary law of personal rights. It is law of a different nature.

With every step towards consolidation, we find the individual threatened in his independence and struggling to set up legal barriers to defend it. It is almost like the beating of a heart. There is a systole in which power is drawn together at the centre and then a diastole in which liberty asserts itself. But it is not exactly like a heart beating. It would be, if each time that heart grew, so that each time the rhythm recurred on a larger scale. It is not simply increase of government, rebellion, increase of government, rebellion, increase of government, rebellion. It is increase of government, rebellion, *adjustment*, increase of government, rebellion, *adjustment*, and so on. After each phase of the politico-social struggle, the two forces of consolidation and freedom arrive at a compromise. Neither defeats the other. The individual surrenders his independence and co-operates socially, for the price of a more and more explicit protection of his personal freedom. From Magna Carta to the Declaration of the Rights of Man, that see-saw between administrative consolidation and individual initiative has gone on. The administration has become progressively more extensive, penetrating and compulsive, the legal defence of liberty more explicit.

That has been the pattern of English history for nearly a thousand years. You could head every page in a text-book of English history, 'The central power grows' or 'The central power is restrained'. The story is complicated by a parallel rhythm between the developing national governments and the Church. Throughout the story, the Church, inheriting the claims of the Empire, is struggling to consolidate a supra-national power in Rome, and the Princes and Kings are making their declarations and defiances, which culminated in the Reformation. Matters of belief enter into that conflict, which led to no general adjustment, but the crude antagonisms of the struggle, growth of organization *versus* liberty, are the same.

The rhythm repeats and complicates itself. The Baron may be protecting himself against the King and at the same time oppressing his underlings. The King may get the better of the Baron by granting charters and protection to the cities, and enlisting their train-bands on his side. But analysed to its final elements it is the same story of the legal protection of the subordinate against the concentrating power. It is the same rhythm.

But now consider how things are with us at present. For the past century and a half there has been a relatively tremendous increase in the administrative scope of governments. Human affairs have been forced towards that unification and simplification of control, that transference of directive power in economic matters from private groups and organizations to a central directorate, which is what we call socialism. Socialism is being forced upon mankind everywhere by forces so nakedly manifest that only people as profoundly miseducated as the British political class can fail to see their significance.

But since the Mandarinate faded out of Chinese affairs, the British academic world and the education it controls have become the most highly organized system of self-complacent backwardness in existence. Repeating once again to these learned gentlemen who, by precept and examination, determine our general education and our popular ideas, the plain facts of the human situation, is almost as hopeful as talking business to a man in a drunken coma or showing photographs to the blind. How well I know it! I have tried to talk the plain A.B.C. of this business to these university people meekly, modestly, apologetically, and I have got nothing but a patronizing smile; tiring at last of that smile, I have tried gross insults, in *Travels of a*

Republican Radical in Search of Hot Water, for example;
I have tried derision in such squibs as *The Camford
Visitation* . . . Once again I will recall the essentials of
the matter, though indeed they are as plain as the sun
of a cloudless noon.

*The abolition of distance and the overwhelming devel-
opment of power in the world during the past century have
rendered uncoordinated political and economic controls
more and more monstrously wasteful and destructive. They
have to be brought together under a collective direction, a
political and economic world order, or our race will blunder
to complete disaster. The whole drift of things is towards
political and economic collectivization, or disaster.*

Surely these three sentences have meaning! But do
they convey anything whatever to the academic or
governing-class mind? Apparently nothing whatever.
They do not even argue about them. They do not seem
to think these statements need to be confuted. 'Look!'
you say, *'collectivism is happening now!'* They just go on,
as automatic as insects. It is like crying 'Fire!' to a
stone-deaf man. The Foreign Offices cling to sover-
eignty and big business clings to its advantages.

Collectivization, with a crude disregard of proprietorship and individual enterprise, has taken possession
of Russia and the totalitarian states, and in the form of
the New Deal it struggles to take possession of

America. With infinite reluctance even the British system to which these government people belong is being forced, backward and protesting, towards the same end. Everywhere we are coming under controls: the rich are being taxed out of power and influence; and yet this system of government, idea-blind, totally unprepared for the task, is under our horrified eyes assuming the management of a new British muddle-headed collectivist state.

That is where we are, and I dare to prophesy that in another score or so of years there will be no governments in the world worth talking about, there will be a mere welter of brigands and gangsters, unless we are all as collectivized as are Russia and the totalitarian states now, and – which is the riddle in the outlook – in some sort of common accord.

That is where the opportunity and responsibility of the Parliamentary peoples and their 'democratic' tradition come in. This collectivism which is rolling down upon us from the East knows nothing of the tradition of personal rights. There have been no Magna Cartas east of the Rhine. It is a collectivization in the dark; even when it is honest it is passionate, dogmatic and impatient of criticism. In the darkness it is bound to blunder into paternalism, absolutism, dishonesty, inefficiency, confusion and disaster.

Hitherto, as I have shown, in our tradition, in our Atlantic world, it has been our usage to meet every increment of centralization with a reassertion of individual liberty. That see-saw between administrative law and fundamental rights which has been our history for centuries has now to be resumed, upon a vaster stage. And with extreme urgency. We could not escape collectivism even if we desired to do so, but we can see to it that it is collectivism in the freedom and the light.

And this time we have to go far beyond that assertion of individual liberty that has hitherto satisfied our ancestors. The new collectivism is taking possession of the entire economic life of the world, and so it is necessary to insist now upon certain claims and rights, that are very generally conceded in practice and sentiment, but which have still to be definitely asserted. The economic factor has to emerge now side by side and merging with the political . . .

This is a brief summary of the principles underlying the next group of clauses of our draft declaration which we shall now consider. In the draft, these claims for the most part precede the political ones. We have put them aside until now because those political claims seemed likely to appeal most immediately to those concerned about the present phase of the world struggle. But now we will go back to the earlier and more fundamental issues. We began our original draft with a very brief exordium followed by a first clause, as follows:

'Since a man comes into this world through no fault of his own, since he is manifestly a joint inheritor of the accumulations of the past, and since those accumulations are more than sufficient to satisfy the claims that are here made for him, it follows:

'(1) That every man without distinction of race or colour is entitled to nourishment, housing, covering, medical care and attention sufficient to realize his full possibilities of physical and mental development and to keep him in a state of health from his birth to death.'

That has since been amended by substituting the words 'without distinction of race, of colour or of professed belief or opinions'. That is to say, there are to be no outcasts at all in the new world order.

A further suggestion by an indignant lady who wanted to insist upon Women's Rights, has been ignored. 'Man' in these Declarations obviously means any living specimen of *Homo sapiens*, male or female, young or old. We regret our constant use of the pronoun 'he', but we did not make the language. The Aryan languages are, we admit, a little over-sexed. If the lady will try substituting 'the individual' and 'the individuals' in our Declaration, and then read it out aloud, she will find it much less satisfying.

Another woman critic demanded a more explicit definition of the rights of parents, the rights of mothers in their children, marital rights and other obligations. Our Declaration, we may note in passing, does as amended give votes to women on exactly the same terms as men, gives them immunity from assault and from restraint, and will, as we shall presently see, protect their property, but we have failed to discover any sort of intersexual behaviour that can be brought within the scope of an elementary Declaration. The nature of the marriage contract, the rights and liabilities of paternity and maternity, how far the community will leave a child under parental control, the protection of minors, the definition and treatment of sexual offences, all fall into the category of administrative legislation and may vary quite conceivably with locality, climate and changing beliefs. There is no reason why particular religious organizations should not have their own special types of contract recognized. It is not a question of elementary liberties.

Magna Carta has a lot to say about wards and heiresses, to remind us of a time when women were still largely chattels. We have grown out of that.

Collectivization has not yet reached, and it may never reach, to a biological control of mankind. The positive eugenics of mankind is a mere speculation of the theorists, and we do not believe that the science of genetics is sufficiently sure of itself, for such negative eugenics as the compulsory sterilization of types capable of transmitting evil hereditable traits. And even if we had that much science, human nature as it is at present revolts against the idea of sterilization without consent. But there is no reason whatever to forbid it to a willing adult who finds his desires at war with his conscience or his happiness.

VII

The Right to Work and to Have Possessions

To a large extent the obligation to provide subsistence, shelter and care is already recognized in practice in the more civilized regions of the earth. Ever since the organization of the Poor Law in England (outcome of More's *Utopia*), there have been food of a sort, shelter of a sort and medical help of a sort for everyone. The quality of this aid has gradually improved. The remnants or rudiments for what that subsistence clause demands are already in existence. All that is demanded is that they be made efficient, world-wide and freed from any suggestion of charity.

These elementary needs can be provided without any great use of money. Few of us realize how many people are now paying a mitigated rent in houses whose building has been subsidized in some way, are getting ninepence for fourpence in their medical attention, are being fed subsidized food. They hike from hostel to hostel which earn no profits: they disport themselves in parks which exact no rent. Few of us, unless we talk to imaginative young architects, have any conception of the sweeping economies and the comforts and beauty that could be effected if we went a step or so further, swept aside the last vestiges of profit and private appropriation and set ourselves as a community to replan and rebuild town and countryside.

It is entirely practicable so to order things that a man may, if he sees fit, go through life without doing a stroke of work, living in a comfortable domicile, walking if he likes from place to place, finding rest homes and free meals wherever he goes, wearing decent clothes. He may lie in the sun and watch the world go by. And why not? The modern community can afford all that now. It may, as William James suggested, conscript him for a year or so, and then he will be free again for the rest of his life. But ———. He will have no pocket money and possibly he may feel a little bored and out of things.

We will come in a paragraph or so to that question of pocket money. But first let us complete the account of the gratuitous services the community will do him, and note also an additional assertion about his freedom.

Clause 2 of our draft Declaration, after certain additions, runs as follows. The additions are put in brackets.

'(2) That he is entitled to sufficient education to make him a useful and interested citizen, [that special education should be so made available as to give him equality of opportunity for the development of his distinctive gifts in the service of mankind,] that he should have easy access to information upon all matters of common knowledge throughout his life and enjoy the utmost freedom of discussion, [association and worship].'

That completes, rather untidily perhaps, the list both of the gratuitous services and of the liberties to which under modern conditions we conceive a man has a legal right. And now we can deal with the right to work and the rights of property, that are necessary to the satisfaction of the restless and creative urgencies in his nature. Clause 5 runs as follows:

'(5) That he may engage freely in any lawful occupation, earning such pay as the need for his work and the increment it makes to the common welfare may justify. That he is entitled to paid employment and to a free choice whenever there is any variety of employment open to him. He may suggest employment for himself and have his claim publicly considered, accepted or dismissed.'

Here money appears upon the scene. A civilized, united and progressive world will be continually replanning itself, rebuilding itself, conducting research, learning, teaching, and thrusting forward into new experiences. It will have to interest and employ a healthy, well-fed population, or face the social dislocation, the possible return to destructive activities and war, its accumulating energy will produce. A large part of the present troubles of our world are due, not to want and insufficiency but to an excess of energy which overflows into war and the preparations and training for war, because we have no other channels ready for it. The monopolization of natural resources by private ownership and private finance, so that the hands of the worker cannot reach them, and the plain necessity for mankind to break through these barriers and liberate these hoarded resources, make such efforts and communism and totalitarianism inevitable. These efforts may be so crude as to blunder at last into war; but until the attack on Finland developed and the mental and moral deterioration of the Soviet Government became manifest, Communism in Russia showed very little disposition for more than precautionary and defensive war. It still seems to be the delusion of the conservative interests in the world that in some way this unchaining of the hoards can be averted. Our subsistence clause very modestly but definitely dispels that dream. 'Tax,' it says in effect to government, 'buy out with money you can presently inflate, or simply appropriate. *These frozen resources must be released.*'

And as the new collectivized state develops the arts and science of management and increases production, it will pay its willing workers in money based on that increasing production, expanding in amount with production, and being in fact no more and no less than a check, giving a call for a definite amount of the surplus products of the community after the elementary requirements of Clause 1 have been satisfied.

And to enforce these ideas, our draft Declaration of Rights proposes the following two clauses, certain aspects of which will necessitate a discussion of the possibility and limits of speculation in a civilized world system. Here are the clauses as they were originally drafted.

'(7) That he shall have the right to buy or sell without any discriminatory restrictions anything which may be lawfully bought or sold, in such quantities and with such reservations as are compatible with the common welfare.'

'(3) That he and his personal property lawfully acquired are entitled to police and legal protection from private violence, deprivation, compulsion and intimidation.'

Are these two clauses as they stand, sufficient to protect the goods of the common citizen from the restless clutch of the dishonest official on the one hand and the entanglements of debt and speculative adventurers on the other?

Free Market and
Profit-Seeking

Let us now repeat what were originally Clauses 7 and 3 in that first draft of the Declaration of Rights in *The Times*. Let us recall them for a closer scrutiny. The rearrangement that this discussion has forced upon us made it fairly plain that these clauses, however they may stand to the personal liberty clauses, need to be grouped together with clause five in the order five, seven, three, thus:

'(5) That he may engage freely in any lawful occupation, earning such pay as the need for his work and the increment it makes to the common welfare may justify. That he is entitled to paid employment and to a free choice whenever there is any variety of employment open to him. He may suggest employment for himself and have his claims publicly considered, accepted or dismissed.'

'(7) That he shall have the right to buy or sell without any discriminatory restrictions anything which may be lawfully bought or sold, in such quantities and with such reservations as are compatible with the common welfare.'

'(3) That he and his personal property lawfully acquired are entitled to police and legal protection from private violence, deprivation, compulsion and intimidation.'

We have to face the realities of human nature; we are discussing a project for a liberal and hopeful world order among our weak and sinful selves and not the prospectus of a millennium. We have to recognize that people will always find a way round a law if there is a way round. We have therefore to consider how we might cheat the good intentions of these provisions.

As the structure of the collectivized state increases in complexity, the opportunities of dictators and high officials in the network of public services, to wangle advantages and reserve this or that desirable thing for their own private gratification will increase and will need to be watched by an alert public opinion. The right of free public criticism will probably keep abuses of this sort within tolerable limits, but it certainly will not abolish the ineradicable craving for advantages. Administrative law may provide pains and penalties for this or that sort of contravention as it becomes flagrant, and that is about all that we can hope to achieve by legislation.

In one respect however our declaration can anticipate a very probable unfairness. What is in view when we talk of property here is individual ownership in a multitude of desirable and delightful things, beautiful books, pictures, objects of art generally, jewels, rare specimens, vintages, exceptional textiles, material for research or artistic work not sanctioned by the administration but sustained by private initiative, exceptionally desirable sites for houses and so on. To obtain all such things many people will be eager to earn money. We have to see that they get their fair choice of things, when they have earned their money.

We will take something very simple and obvious to illustrate the considerations involved. Let us assume there is a peculiar tract of country in the West Indies, which produces tobacco leaf of an exceptional quality which can be manufactured into cigars that a considerable number of people find delightful. It would be an absurd thing for an intelligent administration to do anything else but produce those cigars. How are they to be distributed? An obvious abuse would be for an administration to reserve this brand of cigars for favoured friends either as gifts or as reserved purchases. That can be checked as malversation and embezzlement. The just and proper thing would be to sell them in open market at the maximum price people would offer for them. So far so good.

But now what are we to do if some people want to buy up this brand of cigars not to consume them but with a view to storing them, limiting the release of them and so squeezing up the price that only a few very rich and self-indulgent smokers would be able to get them? Some of the cigars might have to be wasted or destroyed in order that a profit should be made. There is no simple answer to that problem. There is nothing about it we can put into a fundamental law. But that is why we do not declare for an indiscriminate right of purchase in Clause 7. We have to leave it open to administrative law to struggle against such forestalling, regrating and profiteering by regulating sales.

What is said here of cigars applies with equal force to all delightful things, from pearls and precious stones to masterpieces. Even nowadays such things have a general tendency to drift into museums and public galleries and it is a dismal outlook to think of a world where all the loveliness is in corridors behind glass. It has been suggested that many of these things that we want to own and cherish should not be sold but hired out to the highest bidder, who should not be free to sub-let. There is already a Picture Hire company in existence. There may be a considerable check upon buying for profit in this idea.

And when we speak of things being 'lawfully' bought and sold, it is because we have to realize that a very great number of things, stable products, land, productive plant and shipping, for example, will, under the completer phase of collectivization towards which we are moving, be unsaleable and unbuyable. Prospective work may fall under the same restrictions. Joint-stock enterprise is likely to dwindle to very small proportions therefore in that collectivism towards which we are moving. It may in the end prove to have been a quite transitory thing in human experience.

That strange social element in the history of the past three hundred years, the shareholder and the Stock Exchange which still provides him with so much hope and anxiety – mostly anxiety nowadays – may disappear almost altogether. Such organizations as the Unit Trusts of to-day show how easy it would be for the administration to take charge of any money the ordinary man might want to save. Whether it could afford to pay him interest and whether it would compensate him for the secular inflation that must necessarily accompany increasing production, are questions with which I will not complicate the present discussion. I am simply pointing out the reason for the insertion of 'lawfully' in the clauses under discussion.

Nor will I discuss how far a sage world administration would find it necessary to restrain betting and gambling. Most modern governments betray a distrust for this mean form of excitement. Money in a collectivist system is essentially pay for service to the community. It is paid in order that it should be spent either upon the surplus goods produced by the community as a whole, over and above its basic human needs, or else upon those individual private productions that are too questionable or novel or experimental for the administration to undertake. The sooner money is spent upon a product or a service the more it activates the world. The less it is held up or played about with, the better.

Our Declaration of Rights, because of its insistence upon the right to subsistence, makes it impossible for anyone to destroy the freedom of his fellow men by the manipulation of money or property. It is probable that debt will not be allowed to pile up against a man, and payment may be enforced only against those who have received adequate value in service or substance. These are all legislative matters of the third order. We envisage a world in which there will indeed be inequalities between man and man, but none will have power over another, and none will have such a disproportionate fortune as to jostle and humiliate his fellows. It will be a world of infinite variety and incessant change.

Some gambling there will probably be. The individual who finds a zest in playing for money and the charming young person who likes to receive presents, will be with us as long as humanity is humanity. No revolution will rob life of its minor parasitisms, its comedies and petty injustices. Conceivably the turf and the dogs may survive the greatest change in history.

One may doubt whether organized lotteries or betting systems that offer large prizes, are socially desirable, but whatever controls may be necessary in a collectivized state is again a secondary issue.

One other clause of our original draft remains to be noted.

'(6) That he may move freely about the world at his own expense. That his private house or apartment or reasonably limited garden enclosure is his castle, which may be entered only with his consent, but that he shall have the right to roam over any kind of country, moorland, mountain, farm, great garden or what not, or upon the seas, lakes and rivers of the world, where his presence will not be destructive of some special use, dangerous to himself nor seriously inconvenient to his fellow-citizens.'

We have replaced that word 'roam' by two words,

better words they are, from Magna Carta, 'come and go'. So that not only the spirit but some of the very words of that precursor live in this, its latest offspring.

P.S. – But see a further criticism of this clause six at the end of Chapter XI.

IX

The Revised Declaration

The Declaration, revised in accordance with these various suggestions, was tried out upon a number of casually selected people whose reactions were noted. It was pointed out by a shrewd observer that many of them did not seem to realize either its necessity or its far-reaching revolutionary scope, and that as a matter of fact, without my realizing the significance of what I was doing, even when I had sent it to experienced and sympathetic recipients, I had always felt it necessary to recommend it by some sort of justifying preamble. We decided at last that what was at fault was the briefness and dryness of the original exordium.

We had been assuming, which was absurd, that everyone who read it would be as familiar as we were with the concentrated and closely reasoned arguments which had led up to its drafting. We thought that every-one would know and believe what we knew and believed. The Declaration, I may note, even before it went to *The Times*, was sketched out first as part of a book, *The New World Order*, and when it was extracted from that book, we did not realize how much essential matter was left behind. Realizing our mistake at last, we took this exordium in hand and recast it completely, so as to state the quintessence of the human situation which necessitated it. The last thing of this Declaration to be revised, therefore, was its beginning.

The Declaration after this last amendment has been made runs as follows:

Declaration of Rights

'Within the space of little more than a hundred years, there has been a complete revolution in the material conditions of human life. Invention and discovery have so changed the pace and nature of communications round and about the earth that now the distances that formerly kept the states and nations of mankind apart have been practically abolished, and at the same time there has been so gigantic an increment of mechanical power that men's ability either to co-operate with or to injure and oppress one another, and to exploit, consume, develop or waste the bounty of nature, has been exaggerated beyond all comparison with former times. This process of change has mounted to a crescendo in the past third of a century and is now approaching a climax.

'It becomes imperative to adjust man's life and institutions to these increasingly dangerous conditions. He is being forced, almost in spite of himself, to collectivize what was once a patchwork of separate sovereign states and at the same time to rescue his economic life from devastation by the immensely enhanced growth of profit-seeking business and finance. He is doing this clumsily and blindly, and with a great sacrifice of happiness, and well-being. Governments become either openly collectivist under stress of necessity, or they become the instruments of monopolizing financial and business organizations; their power and aggressions increase, they concentrate controls, they subordinate the functions of religious organizations, education and the press to their domination; the direction of scientific and literary work and a multitude of social activities never conceded hitherto to the state, fall into their hands; they are not organized for such purposes; abuses and tyrannies increase, and liberty, and particularly liberty of thought and speech, decays. Throughout the whole world we see variations of this same subordination of the individual to the organization of power. Phase by phase these ill-adapted governments are becoming uncontrolled absolutisms; they are killing

that free play of the individual mind which is the preservative of human efficiency and happiness. The
populations under their sway, after a phase of servile
discipline, are plainly doomed to relapse into disorder
and violence. Everywhere war and monstrous economic exploitation break out, so that those very same
increments of power and opportunity which have
brought mankind within sight of an age of limitless
plenty, seem likely to be lost again, it may be lost for
ever, in an ultimate social collapse.

'It has been the practice of what are called the democratic or Parliamentary countries, to meet every
enhancement and concentration of power in the past,
by a definite and vigorous reassertion of the individual
rights of man. Never before has our occasion to revive
that precedent been so urgent as it is now. We of these
countries recognize the inevitability of the world reconstruction and world collectivism, but after our tradition
we couple with that recognition, a Declaration of
Rights, so that the mighty changes in progress to-day
shall produce not an attempted reconstruction in the
dark, a revolution of disaster, but reconstruction in the
full light of day, a continuing and progressive revolution. To that expedient of a Declaration of Rights, the
outcome of long ages of balance between government

and freedom, we return therefore, but this time upon a world scale, and we declare:

'(1) That every man is joint heir to all the resources, powers, inventions and possibilities accumulated by our forerunners, and entitled without distinction of race, colour or professed belief or opinions, to the nourishment, covering, medical care and attention needed to realize his full possibilities of physical and mental development and to keep him in a state of health from his birth to death.

'(2) That he is entitled to sufficient education to make him a useful and interested citizen, and further that special education should be so made available as to give him equality of opportunity for the development of his distinctive gifts in the service of mankind, that he should have easy access to information upon all matters of common knowledge throughout his life and enjoy the utmost freedom of discussion, association and worship.

'(3) That he may engage freely in any lawful occupation, earning such pay as the need for his work and the increment it makes to the common welfare may justify. That he is entitled to paid employment and to a free choice whenever there is any variety of employment open to him. He may suggest employment for himself and have his claim publicly considered, accepted or dismissed.

'(4) That he shall have the right to buy or sell without any discriminatory restrictions anything which may be lawfully bought or sold, in such quantities and with such reservations as are compatible with the common welfare.

'(5) That he and his personal property lawfully acquired are entitled to police and legal protection from private violence, deprivation, compulsion and intimidation.

'(6) That he may move freely about the world at his own expense. That his private house or apartment or reasonably limited garden enclosure is his castle, which may be entered only with his consent, but that he shall have the right to come and go over any kind of country, moorland, mountain, farm, great garden or what not, or upon the seas, lakes and rivers of the world, where his presence will not be destructive of some special use, dangerous to himself nor seriously inconvenient to his fellow-citizens.

'(7) That a man unless he is declared by a competent authority to be a danger to himself and to others through mental abnormality, a declaration which must be annually confirmed, shall not be imprisoned for a longer period than six days without being charged with a definite offence against the law, nor for more than three months without a public trial. At the end of the latter period, if he has not been tried and sentenced by due process of law, he shall be released. Nor shall he be conscripted for military or any other service to which he has a conscientious objection.

'(8) That although a man is subject to the free criticism of his fellows, he shall have adequate protection from any lying or misrepresentation that may distress or injure him. All administrative registration and records about a man shall be open to his personal and private inspection. There shall be no secret dossiers in any administrative department. All dossiers shall be accessible to the man concerned and subject to verification and correction at his challenge. A dossier is merely a memorandum; it cannot be used as evidence without proper confirmation in open court.

'(9) That no man shall be subjected to any sort of mutilation or sterilization except with his own deliberate consent, freely given, nor to bodily assault, except in restraint of his own violence, nor to torture, beating or any other bodily punishment; he shall not be subjected to imprisonment with such an excess of silence, noise, light or darkness as to cause mental suffering, or to imprisonment in infected, verminous or otherwise insanitary quarters, or be put into the company of verminous or infectious people. He shall not be forcibly fed nor prevented from starving himself if he so desire. He shall not be forced to take drugs nor shall they be administered to him without his knowledge and consent. That the extreme punishments to which he may be subjected are rigorous imprisonment for a term of not longer than fifteen years or death.

'(10) That the provisions and principles embodied in this Declaration shall be more fully defined in a code of fundamental human rights which shall be made easily accessible to everyone. This Declaration shall not be qualified nor departed from upon any pretext whatever. It incorporates all previous Declarations of Human Right. Henceforth for a new era it is the fundamental law for mankind throughout the whole world.

'No treaty and no law affecting these primary rights shall be binding upon any man or province or administrative division of the community, that has not been made openly, by and with the active or tacit acquiescence of every adult citizen concerned, either given by a direct majority vote of the community affected or through the majority vote of his publicly elected representatives. In matters of collective behaviour it is by the majority decision men must abide. No administration, under a pretext of urgency, convenience or the like shall be entrusted with powers to create or further define offences or set up by-laws, which will in any way infringe the rights and liberties here asserted. All legislation must be public and definite. No secret treaties shall be binding on individuals, organizations or communities. No orders in council or the like, which extend the application of a law, shall be enforceable. There is no source of law but the whole people, and since life flows on constantly to new citizens, no generation of the people can in whole or in part surrender or delegate the legislative power inherent in mankind.'

X

A French Parallel

Apt to the moment there comes to hand a *Complément à la Déclaration des Droits de l'homme*, prepared by the *Ligue des Droits de l'homme*, and passed by a Congress of that League at Dijon in July 1936. Our own Declaration was drafted without any knowledge of this *Complément*, and the reader will find it interesting to check back the two. They correspond very closely in their general plan and sometimes they use identical phrases. The French document is rather more plainly feminist and less simply equalitarian in sexual matters. Moreover, it makes a distinction between 'travail' and 'loisirs' which we do not recognize. Nor does it give sufficient value to the forces now making for political collectivization into a world system. It seems rather under the spell of that false analogy which treats of states as only a sort of supra-individual and applies the organizing rules of human intercourse to them, without proper qualifications. We believe much political trouble arises out of this personification of peoples and governments.

This is the text of the document:

'Les Droits de l'Homme, "droits naturels, inaliénables et sacrés", ont été inscrits dans la Déclaration de 1789. Les principes en ont été confirmés et étendus dans le projet de Robespierre, adopté par les Jacobins en avril 1793, at par la seconde Déclaration des Droits, votée par la Convention nationale le 29 mai 1793.

'Ces principes ont fondé la démocratie politique. Mais l'évolution sociale posant des problèmes nouveaux, les progrès des sciences et des techniques permettant des solutions neuves, ces mêmes principes doivent par l'abolition de tous les privilèges fonder la démocratie économique.

'*Article 1*. Les Droits de l'être humain s'entendent sans distinction de sexe, de race, de nation, de religion ou d'opinion.

'Ces droits, inaliénables et imprescriptibles, sont attachés à la personne humaine; ils doivent être respectés en tout temps, en tout lieu et garantis contre toutes les formes politiques et sociales de l'oppression. La protection internationale des Droits de l'Homme doit être universellement organisée et garantie de telle sorte que nul Etat ne puisse refuser l'exercice de ces droits à un seul être humain vivant sur son territoire.

'*Article 2*. Le premier des Droits de l'Homme est le droit à la vie.

'*Article 3*. Le droit à la vie comporte le droit de la mère aux égards, aux soins et aux ressources que nécessite sa fonction – le droit de l'enfant à tout ce qu'exige sa pleine formation physique et morale – le droit de la femme à la suppression intégrale de l'exploitation de la femme par l'homme – le droit des vieillards, malades, infirmes, au régime que réclame leur faiblesse – le droit de tous à bénéficier également de toutes les mesures de protection que la science rend possibles.

'*Article 4*. Le droit à la vie comporte:

'1° Le droit à un travail assez réduit pour laisser des loisirs, assez rémunérés pour que tous aient largement part au bien-être que les progrès de la science et de la technique rendent de plus en plus accessibles, et qu'une répartition équitable doit et peut assurer à tous;

'2° Le droit à la pleine culture intellectuelle, morale, artistique et technique des facultés de chacun;

'3° Le droit à la subsistance pour tous ceux qui sont incapables de travailler.

'*Article 5*. Tous les travailleurs ont le droit de concourir personnellement ou par leurs représentants, à l'établissement des plans de production et de répartition, et d'en surveiller l'application de telle sorte qu'il n'y ait jamais exploitation de l'homme par l'homme, mais toujours juste rémunération du travail et utilisation pour le bien de tous, des puissances de création exaltées par la science.

'*Article 6.* La propriété individuelle n'est un droit que lorsqu'elle ne porte aucun préjudice à l'intérêt commun. L'indépendance des citoyens et de l'Etat étant particulièrement menacée par la propriété qui prend la forme de groupements d'intérêts égoistes et dominateurs (cartels, trusts, consortiums bancaires), les fonctions que cette propriété a usurpées doivent faire retour à la nation.

'*Article 7.* La liberté des opinions exige que la presse et tous les autres moyens d'expression de la pensée soient affranchis de la domination des puissances d'argent.

'*Article 8.* Les fautes commises contre la collectivité ne sont pas moins graves que les fautes commises contre les citoyens.

'Les représentants du peuple et les fonctionnaires investis par la nation d'un pouvoir de direction ou de contrôle sur l'économie, ne peuvent avoir aucun intérêt, accepter aucune place, aucune rémunération, aucun avantage quelconque dans les entreprises qui sont ou ont été soumises à leur surveillance.

'*Article 9.* Toute nation a des droits et des devoirs à l'égard des autres nations avec lesquelles elle constitue l'humanité. Organisée dans la liberté, la démocratie universelle doit être l'objectif suprême des nations.

'*Article 10*. Les Droits de l'Homme condamnent la colonisation accompagnée de violence, de mépris, d'oppression politique et économique.

'Ils n'autorisent qu'une collaboration fraternelle poursuivie en vue du bien commun de l'humanité, dans le plein respect de la dignité personnelle et de toutes les civilisations.

'*Article 11*. Le Droit à la vie implique l'abolition de la guerre.

'*Article 12*. Il n'est pas de circonstance ou un peuple soit excusable d'en provoquer un autre. Tous les différends doivent être réglés soit par la conciliation, soit par l'arbitrage, soit par une juridiction internationale dont les sentences doivent être obligatoires. Tout Etat qui se soustrait à l'observation de cette loi se met en dehors de la communauté internationale.

'*Article 13*. Les nations forment entre elles une société.

'Tout peuple attaqué a le droit d'appeler la collectivité internationale à concourir à sa défense.

'Tous les peuples ont le devoir de se porter au secours du droit violé.

'*Article 14*. Tous ces droits se fondent dans le devoir de la société, qui est de combattre, sous toutes ses formes, la tyrannie – de former des citoyens – de travailler au progrès intellectuel et moral – ainsi qu'au bien-être des individus et des peuples – de leur enseigner l'esprit de paix et la tolérance – et d'appeler sur la terre, à l'exemple de la Révolution française le règne de la raison, de la justice et de la fraternité.'

Being translated this reads as follows:

'The Rights of Man, "natural, inalienable, sacred", were first asserted in the Declaration of 1789. These principles were confirmed and extended in the version by Robespierre adopted by the Jacobins in April 1793 and voted by the National Convention in the Second Declaration of Rights, on May 29th, 1793. But social evolution confronts us with novel problems: the abolition of former privileges and the opening up of fresh solutions by scientific and technical progress now make economic democracy a possible and necessary completion of that former political emancipation.

'*Article 1*. The Rights of a human being are irrespective of sex, race, nationality, religion or opinion.

'These inalienable and imprescribable rights attach to the human personality; they are to be respected on all occasions and everywhere maintained against all political and social oppressions. The world-wide protection of these rights should be so guaranteed that no State should be able to refuse their enjoyment to any human being within its territory.

'*Article 2.* The first right of man is the right to live.

'*Article 3.* The right to live includes the right of the mother to all the care and resources necessary to her function, the right of the child to all that its full moral and physical growth demands, the right of woman to the entire suppression of masculine exploitation, the right of the old, the sick and the infirm to the regime their weakness demands, the right of all to benefit equally in the help and protection that modern science now makes available.

'*Article 4.* The right to live involves also, the right to have work so limited as to leave ample leisure time, and so remunerated that everyone will have a fair share in the well-being which scientific and technical progress renders possible, and an equitable distribution of which could and would now assure to everyone the full intellectual, moral, artistic and technical development of all his or her faculties and a sufficient subsistence for everyone incapable of work.

'*Article 5.* All workers have the right to participate, either personally or through their representatives, in the planning of production and distribution, and to supervise the operation of such planning so as to prevent the exploitation of man by man and so as to secure the just rewards of labour and the fullest utilization for the good of all of the scientifically exalted bounty of nature.

'*Article 6.* Private property is only a right when it does not infringe upon the common interest. The independence of the nation and its citizens is now more particularly threatened by aggressive proprietary interests (cartels, trusts and banking controls) and it becomes of primary importance to restore these usurped powers to the common weal.

'*Article 7.* Liberty of opinion demands that the press and all other media of thought and expression should be released from the control of monetary power.

'*Article 8.* Infringements of the rights of the community as a whole, are as grave as the infringement of individual rights. No representatives of the people and no functionaries entrusted by the nation with the direction and controls of economic life, should be allowed to derive any profit in, or accept any place, remuneration or advantage whatsoever, in the interests which have been entrusted to their care.

'*Article 9.* All nations have rights and duties towards their fellow nations, which collectively constitute humanity with them. Universal democracy, organized in freedom, should be the supreme objective of all nations.

'*Article 10.* The Rights of Man condemn colonization involving violence, debasement and political and economic oppression. They recognize only the possibility of brotherly collaboration in the service of human welfare, conducted with the fullest respect for human dignity and civilized standards of behaviour.

'*Article 11*. The right to live implies the abolition of war.

'*Article 12*. There are no circumstances which justify one people's provoking another. All differences should be settled either by conciliation, arbitration, or by an international jurisdiction whose decisions are authoritative and final. Every State which disregards that law puts itself outside the community of nations.

'*Article 13*. The nations of the earth constitute a society. Every people suffering from aggression has the right to appeal to the human collectivity for defence, and it is the duty of all peoples to go to the aid of violated national rights.

'*Article 14*. All these rights merge in the duty of society as a whole to combat every form of tyranny, to form citizens, to work for the well-being not only of individuals and societies but for moral and intellectual progress, to inculcate the spirit of peace and tolerance and to spread throughout the entire world, in accordance with the great tradition of the French Revolution, the reign of reason, justice and universal brotherhood.'

To inspire a movement, to stir meetings, to quote, this type of declaration is certainly very effective, but as a weapon in the hands of some obstinate lawyer, like my friend W. H. Thompson for example, fighting a case in a police court – and that is where thousands of battles for freedom will have to be fought – or a member of Parliament pursuing some unrestrained legislator, we believe our own is the tougher, more practicable instrument.

XI

An Alternative Draft and Some Further Suggestions

Here next, by way of stimulus to discussion is another draft of a Declaration, emanating from the 'Cambridge Peace Aims Group', which appears to be mainly Mr Robert Jordan. It runs as follows:

'Charter of the Rights and Duties of Modern Man

'Here are the Rights:

'(i) FOOD. Every man shall be entitled to sufficient food to give him the fullest nutrition to develop his physique to the fullest capacity and to play his full part in the life of the community.

'(ii) HEALTH. Every man shall be entitled from conception till death to benefit from the best medical and surgical achievements of the day and to the fullest enjoyment of hygienic and preventive services.

'(iii) ENVIRONMENT. Every man shall be entitled to housing with services and equipment, to surroundings favourable to all his activities and generally to an ordered environment, whether urban or rural, in accordance with the best planning principles of the day.

'(iv) EDUCATION. Every man shall be entitled to a sound and objective education and there shall be genuine equality of opportunity. Education shall be a matter of environment as well as of instruction, and everyone shall be entitled to an education untouched by the interests of any party or religion.

'(v) FREEDOM. Every man shall be entitled to as much freedom as is compatible with the freedom of others. He shall have full freedom of thought, speech, assembly and movement about the world without passport or visa. He shall be free to live and work where he chooses (subject only to the regulations of the world labour bureau). Every man shall have his home and property secured against entry or confiscation by others, and he shall possess such literature, etc., as he chooses. He shall have access to all open spaces except such as are set aside with each house for private use, provided, of course, such access does not interfere with industrial or agricultural processes. No man shall own property of such a quantity or character as shall involve the exploitation of others. Every man shall have the right to buy or sell such commodities as may be lawfully traded with such reservations as are necessary for the common good. No man shall be imprisoned any-where in the world for more than a short stated period without open public trial, and he shall then have free legal advice and full knowledge of the process of appeal available to him. No man shall be subject to spying or enforced exile. When convicted of any crime he shall be subject at the most to imprisonment under hygienic con-ditions. (Without here entering into details, crime shall be regarded pathologically – a disease to be cured or prevented.) There shall be no political crimes on the stat-ute book. Every man shall be entitled to have access to all Truth which is humanly obtainable, and no measures shall be taken to withhold from him any facts or opinions or to prevent him publishing any facts or opinions.

'And here are the Duties:

'Every man shall (in accordance with his mental and physical capacity) do some work which shall either dir-ectly or indirectly benefit the community. He shall not be compelled to do unpleasant or undignified work for more than the minimum number of hours which equal distribution and scientific devices shall make possible. Every man shall be entitled to public consideration of his claim to do such work as is in accordance with his in-clinations or interests. No man shall hold any post or public appointment except on the grounds of his ability.

'Every man or organization who, by reason of

research or experiment or special ability, shall achieve, discover or invent something which might benefit others shall publish the results of such work and shall be suitably rewarded.

'Every man shall perform such necessary civic duties as voting, sitting on juries, etc., and such other voluntary work as may from time to time be required of him for the general good.

'THESE RIGHTS AND DUTIES OF MAN SHALL BE THE CONCERN OF THE WHOLE WORLD, AND IT SHALL BE THE FIRST DUTY OF THE SUPREME GOVERNMENT TO GUARANTEE THEM TO ALL MEN EVERYWHERE. THE SUPREME GOVERNMENT SHALL BE ENTITLED TO STEP IN AND ACT, IF NECESSARY WITH THE AID OF FORCE, IF ANY LOCAL GOVERNMENT IS FAILING IN ITS DUTY TO PROVIDE MAN WITH HIS ELEMENTARY AND FUNDAMENTAL RIGHTS OR TO ADMINISTER A STRICT ENFORCEMENT OF THE LAW IN ACCORDANCE WITH FUNDAMENTAL ABSTRACT JUSTICE.'

(i), (ii), (iii) and (iv) are in effect our Clauses 1 and 2. It is for the reader to decide which is the better wording. In (v) and the 'Duties', which are more or less the equivalent of the rest of our Declaration, there is a certain excessiveness of assumption: the existence of a 'world labour bureau', for example, and the assertion that 'crime is to be regarded as primarily pathological'. Many people, the present writer included, believe there is quite a lot of normal and incurable wickedness in mankind which has to be restrained. At any rate, it seems unnecessary to raise the issue. The Clause about passports and visas appears inadvisable to me. It will surely be necessary for a man to carry some sort of identification papers in a world community, and this clause seems, I say *seems*, to exonerate him from doing so. Upon one or two points (v) is compacter than our draft, but I have given reasons, based on the Magna Carta precedent, for overflowing occasionally into detail and pointing explicitly at present evils.

The duties of 'sitting upon a jury and voting' are not mentioned in our Declaration. I do not think, myself, that a man should be obliged to vote upon any issue. He has, I maintain, a right to tacit acquiescence. 'Trial by jury' in a world of open criticism and discussion, may be a much less necessary guarantee of liberty than it was in the small untravelled, illiterate communities of the past. A recording microphone, cameras, alert critical reporters, unrestrained publicity, may provide a check upon the unjust magistrate more efficiently than any boxful of 'twelve good men and true'. The proviso, in the Cambridge draft, that 'every man *shall* perform . . . voluntary work' is no doubt a slip of the pen.

Among other criticisms to which our Declaration has been subjected is first of all the use of the word 'Revolution' in the third paragraph of the exordium. The objection is a practical one. A great number of people have been trained to regard 'Revolution' as meaning a dreadful destructive breaking-up of social ties, with barricades, tumbrils and so on, and why should they be shocked by such a word? I see no strong reason why their fear should not be dispelled by substituting 'world reconstruction' for 'world revolution', though I believe that as far as possible people should be induced to think rather harder than they do about the real meaning of the words they use.

Moreover, and quite another matter, in Clause 6, the experienced police official will object at once to the immunity of the 'Englishman's castle'. There are certain cases, he will insist, that justify a search warrant. Search may be necessary when dealing with certain forms of criminality, but it is very easy to abuse the right of search. I would like to have that particular sentence recast ultimately in consultation with an expert criminologist or so, and some one from Scotland Yard. I find it difficult to devise the sort of qualifying phrase needed for this occasion, and I can find no one with anything to suggest. And I would like at the same time to have a conference with the same committee upon Clause 8 about the right of a man to see and challenge his dossier. It has been suggested that every professional criminal will be demanding a sight of his dossier to discover just exactly what the police know about him. I doubt that. I do not see Bill Sikes or a suspected poisoner or forger going to the record office and sitting down to have a frank talk with two or three detectives about his past and present. He might give away more than he got. As a trial amendment I suggest the following revised clause:

'That although a man is subject to the free criticism of his fellows, he shall have adequate protection from any lying or misrepresentation that may distress or injure him. The substantial facts in all dossiers kept for administrative purposes, shall be accessible to the man concerned and subject to verification or correction at his challenge. A dossier is merely a memorandum for administrative use; it may justify temporary detention subject to the provisions of the preceding clause, but neither deportation nor any other penalties; it cannot be used as evidence without proper confirmation in open court.'

But that still leaves me in the air about that search warrant. Suppose we were to add to Clause 6: 'Or by a legally qualified person empowered by a warrant as the law may direct?'

Here perhaps is the place for another afterthought.

It has been suggested that one single Declaration of

Rights may not be adapted to all occasions. The World State, like the Christian Church, might well have a shorter and a longer creed. And like the French Revolution, the World Revolution might very well embody its primary idea in a slogan. The French slogan was Liberty, Equality and Fraternity. This seems to need only one addition. We want to emphasize 'equality of opportunity'. Perhaps 'Liberty, Fraternity, Equality of Opportunity, and Equality Before the Law' would be a suitable amendment.

I find it very difficult to turn my mind from the elaboration of a full Declaration to the production of any simple formula, which would express our revolutionary purpose in a comprehensive manner and at the same time leave no loopholes for effective evasion. Something on the lines of the Declaration of Independence may be possible. 'I believe in the right of every living human being, without distinction of colour, race, sex or professed belief or opinion, to liberty, life and subsistence, to complete protection from ill-treatment, equality of opportunity in the pursuit of happiness and an equal voice in the collective government of mankind. For those primary rights, for others and myself, I am prepared to struggle with all my strength and ability whenever I am called upon to do so.' Does that say enough?

XII

The New Map of the World

This book is concerned with the Declaration of Rights which is the proper and necessary response of the Atlantic civilizations to the swiftly advancing need for a social and economic collectivization. It concentrates on that.

I will not argue here whether this Declaration embodies the spirit of Christianity or owes anything to Christianity, or debate any side issues of that kind. Some correspondents declare it *is* simply Christianity. Many Roman Catholics attack its fundamental ideas ferociously. I shall be only too glad to discover that it is Christianity, and, though I do not profess Christianity, to work side by side for these ends with those who do. And also if it is claimed that this embodies the spirit of Islam, Judaism, Buddhism, Bahism or any other -ism, I do not mind. Whoever accepts the Declaration is my ally and fellow citizen. I will not discuss beliefs that stand that test here. Nor will I take up here that other aspect of our world situation, and attempt to demonstrate the commanding need for a collectivization of human affairs. I have dealt with that as compactly and fundamentally as I can in *The Fate of Homo sapiens* and in *The New World Order*. I cannot compress those very concentrated arguments further.

Plainly I am an extreme revolutionary. Although I dislike rhetoric and emotion intensely, my reason nevertheless compels me to be extreme. I do not believe it is possible to go on with the present way of living that prevails throughout the world, with the sovereign governments we have and the economic practices that prevail. These sovereign governments have given us nothing but inconclusive wars on a larger and larger scale, and we have to get rid of them all. All of them. It is not the present German Government we are fighting to get rid of; it is any government of that sort, including most emphatically our own. We have to get rid of and replace all these governments by a world system, and that alone is world revolution. But, in addition, we have to get rid of and replace methods of exploiting natural advantages, business control and finance, that in the midst of possible plenty keep nearly all of us poor and needy, sweated and bored. This applies equally to the maladministration of Russia and the Totalitarian states and the chaotic scramble for profit of the so-called capitalist countries. All in their various ways waste and devastate life. The common sense of mankind revolts against these things and grows less and less patient with them.

This has become plainer and plainer in our minds as the years have passed. More and more of us realize that we have to assemble our affairs in a new and far better unifying organization or pass on to complete social disintegration. We are suffering in a sluggish and incomplete revolution, because it is sluggish and unwilling and inadequate. Because revolutionary movements have failed and have been frustrated hitherto that is no argument against revolution. It is an argument for a bolder and better revolution.

For decades the political and revolutionary unrest of the world has wasted itself upon unsound and insufficient formulæ, of which the League of Nations idea and Stalinized-Leninized-Marxism are typical samples. Neither of these schemes, which the conflicts of 1914–18 released, was thought out soundly and boldly enough; they have brought us to where we are; they gain nothing in dignity by the fact that their failure has been world-wide, bloody and costly both in time and in human happiness. The League of Nations is evidently giving place in many men's hopes and imaginations now to what is at present an even more unsubstantial and uncreative gesture, the Federation idea. Something may be made of it perhaps; but at present it is no better than a pious aspiration. In *The New World Order* I have shown how provisional and unsubstantial it is, and how much needs to be added to it before it should be urged upon people, even as a first step towards world rationalization. Communism as a project for a new world order I have also subjected in the same book to a destructive statement of the obvious. Both these things equally – League-of-Nationism and Communism – have lost heart and failed. We can never go back to them. They are over and we have to go on.

But it is no longer necessary to explode the pretensions of Communism to world leadership. They have been exploded for all time by Mr Molotov, the Russian Foreign Minister. He has declared that the U.S.S.R. has its own 'ideology' and will not interfere with the 'ideologies' of other states. There for the present Russia closes its revolutionary story. With these words the U.S.S.R. becomes no more than a nationalized imperialism and resigns whatever pretensions it has ever had to revolutionary leadership in the world. The Communists who work for it in other countries become now simply the propaganda agents of a foreign power.

So the ideas of fundamental world reorganization and ultimate world unity return for a phase of refreshment and renewal to the lands and peoples among whom they were originally begotten. We of the Western World who think and speak freely have to take up the one world revolution where Stalin and Molotov have laid it down. Without slogans or claptrap we must go on now to rally the shattered forces of human reconstruction. The battle for world regeneration enters upon a new phase. These first waves of attack have gone as far as they can do; they await reinforcement and a new formation.

Socialization is a process intricate in detail, many-sided and variable. I have done my best to take a general view of it in *The New World Order*. But this Declaration of Rights is the absolutely necessary implement for holding together and controlling all those operations of expropriation, re-appropriation and so forth and so on, which are essential to the great change. An absolutely necessary implement. And it is possible to bring it into effective operation forthwith. You can put this book down and begin. Everywhere groups and individuals can press it upon the attention of their Parliamentary candidates and representatives, their social and political organizations, their public leaders, their administrations and governments. They can insist. They can say: 'Is this what you stand for, and if not, why not? Why are you not accepting it? Tell us explicitly what there is in it you will not support. Or we will refuse to trust you. We will denounce. We will distrust and denounce and defeat whatever you are doing.'

In quite a little while this draft declaration, which really, radical though it is, contains nothing new or startling, which does simply get together and embody in one plain statement general ideas practically operative and active in our democratic communities, can be made the explicit criterion of our war aims and the ruling idea of all our efforts. It can pull us all into shape. Once it is fairly launched, it will go about the world. It will insist upon itself. It will go into neutral and enemy countries. It will find allies for us there and everywhere. Once it has begun to be printed and reprinted and discussed, it will defy any censorship. Nobody can claim a restrictive copyright in a statement of fundamental public importance, so ordered and compact. It will become the backbone of the new revolution everywhere.

We can then, with this declaration as a common basis, turn to all this swelling literature about Federation and all the proposed new maps of Europe, and the whole tangled problem of war aims, with some hope of practicable solutions. Either governments will set themselves firmly against the Declaration and do what they can to suppress it, and so become the open enemies of the new world order, or they will accept it, and by so doing align themselves with the forces of rational world reconstruction as provisional administrations on the way to a world system, or they will attempt to ignore it. But if a sufficient clamour for a Declaration of Rights is maintained, they will ignore it with a deepening sense of dishonesty and guilt. The only governments to which a rational man can now give even provisional allegiance are governments which have accepted this Declaration of Rights, or a Declaration essentially similar, as their basic political law, which are con-sciously provisional and confessedly doing their work in trust for the world pax.

Now if the people who, inspired by Mr Clarence K. Streit's *Union Now*, are talking seriously of a Federal system in the world and not merely making optimistic noises of no value whatever, then they propose a repe-tition, on a larger scale, of the developmental method of the United States of America, which consisted of a growing number of fully organized federated States plus a number of territories not yet properly and satis-factorily equipped to take an equal place in the Federal Union but destined finally to full state status. So evi-dently the aim of these federalists, if they are the least bit sincere, involves *the dissolution of the French and*

British imperial systems into a constellation of states and territories and the association with them of a number of now neutral countries which have agreed to accept the same collectivist principles and the same organization into states and probationary territories. And it means also *the reduction of the British monarchy to a merely formal survival*. If you are not prepared for these preliminaries, then in the name of common sense stop shouting 'Federation'.

These federated states, we are told, are to have a common money, which is only possible with a common property and money system, they are to have unrestricted free trade and a complete pooling of their military, naval and air armament and organization. All that is proposed, a little indistinctly perhaps, but quite definitely, in *Union Now*. All that I do in my various criticisms of Mr Streit is to ask him not to mumble. The utmost military organization a state will possess will be a state militia for the preservation of internal order. Either these federalists have squared their minds up to all this, or their talk is empty babble only fit for a vicarage tea-party.

But since, for the reasons we have italicized in an earlier section, the world becomes one, this Federal Union idea cannot be confined to any group of states, however extensive. It has to be propagandist for all the world. The 'abolition of distance' means in practice the abolition of boundaries. An act of gross cruelty or injustice that occurs in Manchuria or Danzig is as much an Englishman's concern now, as if it occurred in Nigeria or Cardiff. Nowadays the infection of such evils travels too fast to be ignored. In only a week of years, as we have seen, a terroristic gangsterism can develop from back-street outrages to a savage and dangerous assault upon the peace of mankind. We need to bring all the world into our map of states and territories.

Streit talks in his book of the United States of Europe, makes the United States of America one of the 'founder states', but hesitates to bring Russia or Eastern Asia into his schemes. Sooner or later, and sooner rather than later, they must come in. It may be that as a transitional phase there may be secondary groupings of the Oslo Powers or the Latin Union or the Balkan Powers, but such groupings must be confessedly on the way to the ultimate synthesis, and they will not be safely adjusted until that synthesis is complete.

The ultimate pattern of world government to which human affairs move seems to be a combination of the collectivist ideal, the state socialism of Russia, *plus* a rigorous insistence upon the Declaration of Rights we have set out here. East is East and West is West, and the sooner they get together the better. The U.S.S.R. is a federal system. Moscow deals with the common staple productions, money, transport, and so forth, but there is a wide variety of constituent states under that central control. For matters of local administration it is obviously more convenient to keep together peoples using the same language and having common cultural traditions. Let us hope all the states develop their own architecture, for example. The federal government and the world common law will be the joint protectors of entangled minorities and of the passing stranger, in the more intensely patriotic areas.

This being the pattern at which we aim, the policy of a rational man will be towards setting up a state in the federal union wherever such a natural solidarity is to be found. Our first 'War Aim' will be to secure the acceptance of the Declaration of Rights from as many potential states as possible. Our second should be to facilitate their groupings according to race, kindred and local preference, whenever they desire it, for their cultural association and protection against the swamping influence of larger systems, keeping always in mind the supremacy of the common law. A case in point would be the various Slav-speaking states from Bohemia to Poland and Serbia, who might prefer to base their intellectual development upon Russian rather than German. The present French and British

Governments have made large, vague promises to 'restore' Czechoslovakia and Poland, apparently to their original boundaries. But both of these, when they were over-run, were artificial political systems. Bohemia is a fairly real country, Poland to the extent of the old Grand Duchy of Warsaw or a little beyond; they have every right to be states and to delay and choose their federal associates when they feel like it. But wild pledges by the Allied Governments are no more to be respected than any secret treaties they may be making now. We, the people, have not been consulted. They are not our concern. Which is one reason among many why there has to be a change of governments in the 'democratic' allies quite as much as in Germany before there can be any pretence of a European peace settlement.

Meanwhile the war against militant Germany must go on.

There are a number of tender-hearted people who do not wish to see Berlin bombed or the common Germans experiencing any of the miseries that they have allowed their Government to inflict on other nations. I do not share this excessive tenderness for the German people, nor do I believe a vigorous bombing and so forth would do anything to embitter them against us. They believe themselves to be a brave military race;

they evidently feel ruthlessness is a permissible quality in righteous anger; at every opportunity they swagger about, singing heroic songs and kicking their inferiors; and they deny vigorously that they were beaten, as they were beaten, in 1918. They seem to have an ineptitude for reality until it is made extremely real to them. It is, I believe, a misfortune for all mankind that Berlin was not soundly bombed, as it could have been, in 1918.

The Germans have shown very little regard for the sufferings their belligerence has inflicted on millions of people outside their borders, and, when one has weighed all the possible excuses that can be made for them, it still remains against them that in a quarter of a century they have twice marched enthusiastically behind ruthlessly aggressive leaders. Do these heroic warriors really want to be treated with mawkish consideration directly the scales of war tilt against them? Must they go on for ever in alternate phases of war and whining? Would it not rather conduce to a manly mutual respect if, as people say, we gave it to them hot and good?

They have insisted on being a nuisance to all the world, they have stopped the wheels of progress, life is entirely disorganized not only in France and England and Poland but in Sweden, Holland, Belgium, on account of their love for playing soldiers, and it is absurd to concentrate upon Herr Hitler the responsibility for all that fierce, fatuous, crowd-swaggering which thousands of photographs have recorded. There are thousands of pictorial records. There are, I say, many excuses for the Germans, Versailles and the strangulation after 1919–20, etc., etc. – we all know how sound their excuses are, we concede them almost excessively, we over-do it; none the less they have been made excuses for abominable behaviour – and I am convinced that vigorous bombing and bombarding, town-wrecking and the like, would be an entirely wholesome and chastening experience for the German 'soul'.

It has been for us. Navy-proud Englishmen have never had quite the same feeling about marine bombardments since the shelling of Scarborough, and Mr Anthony Eden, who opposed the abolition of the bombing plane by the League of Nations, probably sees that weapon now from quite a new angle. One object lesson, one home lesson, in such things is worth endless hearsay, as any leader will testify.

Germans have to see and feel for themselves as recipients, the heroic blonde mothers and that heroic blond little boy, the Nazi kicker of to-morrow, have to feel in their own skins what sort of war it is they have made and applauded in Poland, for example. It is far better than blockade and starvation, more impressive, less drawn-out and less easily explained away. Let them run and cower and like it.

Unless the war passes into such a phase of recognizable defeat for Germany at home, I see little probability of any war end that will be more than an interval for German recuperation and rearmament. As Count Ciano has recently explained with perfect frankness, 'peace' to the National Totalitarian State means a phase of recovery between aggressive wars. The devastated regions of France and Belgium have not made the French and Belgians into war fanatics. On the contrary they have made them extraordinarily thoughtful about war. The Germans would be all the better for similar regions in their home land to meditate upon.

I make these unusual, these un-Quakerlike, remarks without any feeling of vindictiveness towards Germans. I am a pacificist, but I am a realistic pacificist. I want an organized world peace. But I have always thought it a mean way of scoring off an antagonist to turn the other cheek. It is disrespectful to his pugnacity, it is irritatingly smug, and much more likely to stir him up to further outrage than to turn his wrath aside. Let the Germans have their medicine now. I maintain that the nett saving in human life and the increased security of the next generation of human beings all about the earth, would enormously outweigh the suffering that would have to be inflicted in order to demonstrate to these people just what being a Nazi involves for others – and ultimately for themselves. I believe the Germans are potentially one of the greatest peoples upon the face of the earth; I am altogether opposed to any diplomatic arrangements that would cut up their natural great community into small, sterilized states. It is a valuable and important population of immense scientific and literary capabilities, which has now to be restored, even by drastic means, to health. There is no real alternative to a healthily beaten Germany but some diplomatist's scheme for perpetual enfeeblement and discord in the heart of Europe that will be far worse for the general human outlook.

Germany, I insist, has to be beaten and disarmed, and I see no reason to recoil from the idea of that's involving some rough times for her, not enfeebling and miserable times, but rough times; she has to go through with that; and then I think we ought to accept some genuine German scheme for her general future. We ought not to have some Congress of the Powers mapping things out for her, but we ought to put it severally to the ancient divisions of the German Confederation, Prussia, Bavaria, Saxony, Austria, and so on, to accept the Declaration of the Human Rights they have ignored and to decide how far they will remain separate, and how far they will federate up to the limit of a single, complete, German-speaking community, unified politically, economically and intellectually, and how far, severally or altogether, they will come into any wider federal system. That is their affair. But it is the affair of the whole world that they should cease to march and arm.

Very probably the Weimar Constitution, which is still legally the fundamental law of Germany, may be a suitable instrument for the restoration of legality in Germany, just as there may be dormant possibilities of liberalization in the Russian Constitution of 1936. These are questions I have not had the necessary opportunity to examine. But in such a phase of conflict and confusion as lies before us there can be little question of the steadying value of such precedents and revivals in which a nation can recognize its own spontaneous will rather than the compulsion of the foreigner.

There could be no better factor in a reconstituted world than a demilitarized Germany released from her present puerile malignancy. The more she is 'let off' the realities of defeat, the more she will resent it and lie about it. We want these eighty millions to grow up to a sober and chastened partnership in the world's affairs.

Germany has to be disarmed, as all the world has to be disarmed, and it is absurd to talk of 'leaving her alone to herself'. There was an extraordinary mass of foolish talk after 1918 about not interfering in the internal affairs of this, that or the other member of the League of Nations. It is time we recognized fully that the making of any lethal weapon larger than what may be required for the control of big animals, is a matter of universal concern, just as aggressively nationalistic history text-books or the fostering of infectious diseases in swamps and slums, or interference with free speech, is a matter of universal concern. Making a weapon, except for unavoidable police necessity, making a provocative lie anyhow, or fostering fever, is the first stage in murder. Whatever federal systems we contemplate as we draw the map of our future world, are systems that will have a very definite and reasonable aggressiveness. They will need police organization in common not only for mutual reassurance but to control as far as possible what is going on outside the federal boundaries. The coalescence of such international police forces, once they exist and prove their usefulness, into a world system, may go on very rapidly. On the one hand it may be found convenient to entrust air and sea control to such an organization, and on the other it might even keep an eye upon educational reaction.

The ending of warfare will put no stop to the mental conflicts of mankind. We have heard a lot in the past two decades of communist propaganda in the West; we shall hear, I hope, even more of liberal propaganda in the East. We can adopt very parallel methods, and though the propaganda in Russia of the Declaration of Rights by actual democratic governments (when we get them) might be an embarrassment in such international relations as survive, a propaganda by organizations enjoying the liberties of democratic institutions is an altogether different matter. The nearer we approach to the abolition of war and of the nationalist use of force and economic pressure, the more intense the conflict and competition of languages and types of culture may become. Instead of subsidized spy systems and propagandas, we may have the organized endowment of university chairs, presses, periodicals, special schools, exhibitions and theatres . . .

But we will not wander too far along the road to Utopia. This little book begins and ends to advocate a renewal of the Declaration of the Rights of Man as an instrument of primary necessity and importance in the adjustment of human affairs to that world collectivism which is overtaking the entire planet.

XIII

A Book for Which the World Is Waiting

At present all sorts of able people in the English-speaking countries and France are writing books with the burthen *It must never happen again*. In France this usually means nothing more or less than as complete a destruction of Germany as possible. They have the strongest justification for this grim resolve. From '71 onward Germany has made herself intolerable to France, and it is hard to ask a Frenchman now – or a Pole or a Czech or a Dane or a Hollander or a Belgian – to entertain the possibility of trusting a Germany so changed as to be a good European state. They can scarcely be expected to accept anything but a Germany completely disarmed, competently policed against secret rearmament, garrisoned at strategic points and politically and culturally broken up. It is that breaking-up I find distasteful and impossible. The rest I accept. The more a people reads, the more its language consolidates it. Except for that breaking-up of Germany, I am at one with the French radicals.

Now how is the effacement of Germany to be averted and at the same time the reasonable fears of her injured and menaced neighbours to be dispelled? Only by the emergence of a Liberal Germany, willing to accept defeat and disarmament provided it is left free to develop its distinctive cultural unity.

I went to Stockholm last September mainly to get hold of Mr Thomas Mann and work out some common statement with him, about world affairs. I thought if we could get something fundamental in common, our two peoples could. But I could get nothing out of him. And since then I have been trying to establish contacts with intellectual Germans (who must obviously be 'Aryans') who would produce that book I need, *It must never happen again*, in German first, and then put into English and French, so that they come frankly into line with the forces of world reconstruction. There are Germans who can see things clearly. Could they not accept our conception of human rights and produce a Manifesto in the spirit of this letter with which I conclude this book? The letter runs as follows:

'Dear Mr Wells,

'Your question was: what wish the Intellectuals for a future Germany?

'I shall try to answer as shortly and distinctly as possible.

'The foremost interest of the German Intellectuals is a state of affairs in which the Rights of Men – of whom you gave recently an admirable new interpretation – are secured.

'In the following considerations I presume that Hitlerism will be crushed soon.

'From which parties who offer themselves for his succession can we expect that our claims will be respected?

'From the beginning I may exclude here the Communist party and the National Bolshevik party. Both, it is true, talk much of "freedom". Yet, we know that they use the word in another sense than we do it.

'Further on there offers herself one group which affirms at least to be backed by parts of the General Staff. To this apparently are belonging: Rauschning, Brüning, Treviranus, and that part of the Social Democrat Party which is represented by the old "Parteivorstand" (Executive Committee), now in Paris. From the point of the Intellectuals one has every reason to mistrust such a combination. (By the way: also from the point of lasting peace.) The General Staff will not change its traditional character, and indeed it always was directed against the Liberal Rights. In such a combination the armed forces would be stronger than those parties allied to them. Thus, what would to be expected would be an autocratic regime supported by the trade unions, preparing carefully and with better manners a new war, rather than a Parliamentary government and Freedom of the press and of science and learning. Yet, it should not necessarily be impossible, especially if the disarmament would be more energetically enforced than the last time, that the development would go contrary to the wishes of the Army officers.

'Secondly, there will be some groups calling themselves socialist but actually rather communist though hostile to Moscow. They also will promise freedom. But also towards them every distrust will be legitimate. They speak of "economic planning", and what they mean is scarcely something different from a centralized economic administration which is doomed to lead fast to a totalitarian system. Yet, these people deserve support in the case that the sooner mentioned group (Rauschning, etc.) would come into office. In this case those genuine socialists would have the interest in upkeeping freedom for themselves and consequently as well for others.

'There will reappear after Hitler's defeat the Catholic Centre Party. They have members who are not trustworthy, as for instance Brüning, who always acted alone in the interests of the General Staff and feels himself much more as army-man than as catholic. But in general the Catholics are trustworthy. They are a minority, at least in the Bismarckian Reich, without Austria. They have been persecuted by the old Prussia in the 'forties, then again by Bismarck and now by Hitler. Therefore they know that they have to support intellectual freedom for their own sake, and one can rely on them to a large extent.

'Much can be done for us Intellectuals by the peace treaty; after a renewed defeat, the second in 25 years, the influence of the victorious Powers will be enormous including their example. Yet, it is very difficult for them to understand their task, especially because what we need is a mixture of socialist and of capitalist measures. We need the liquidation of the large Eastern estates for economic reasons but foremost for political reasons. They always were the stronghold of the Junkers, and indeed the Junkers were the people who finally gave the power to Hitler. This liquidation is easily done. It is only necessary to prevent *every* kind of economic protection for the production of corn. Then they will be ruined what they have deserved, from every point, since 150 years. Secondly we need nationalization of the coal and iron industry. Their owners are the old allies of the Junkers (since the beginning of the protective tariff policy in 1878), they supported Hitler and will again support every attempt of authoritarian regime. Finally they are, from the economic point, not only useless but actually damaging. As they cannot live without protective tariffs enforced free trade will endanger them earnestly. Yet, it would be better and more secure to take them over by the State.

'On the other hand it is, always from the point of the Intellectuals, absolutely necessary to keep up the general principle of a free market. In every economically centralized or totalitarian system liberty would be smashed soon.

'There exists hardly a party acting directly in the interest of the Intelligentsia. The Democratic Party had nearly disappeared before Hitler rose to power. The Liberals, who had been so strong in the 'sixties and 'seventies, had become, to a large extent, the servants first of Bismarck and Wilhelm II, then of every kind of nationalist reaction and of war preparation. However, they now have been taught a lesson. From some examples I met in Oxford I should think they now understand better what liberty and law means for them, and I earnestly hope professors, lawyers, and doctors will behave more sensibly and less nationalist-romantically than they have done before. If this is so it should be possible to build up again a Liberal or Democratic Party, which, in close contact with the Catholic Party, could possibly have a strong influence.

'At last there remain two questions: dismemberment and monarchy.

'I do not think partition of Germany could serve any good aim. It would, unavoidably, lead to a new nationalist movement for unity and would absorb all good forces in a useless struggle.

'Secondly, monarchy? I do not mind in principle. But who is a candidate? Apparently only the Hohenzollerns. They are the traditional war-lords, chiefly supported by the Army, and should therefore be excluded from any kind of political activity.

'The failures of Versailles should be avoided, the assets repeated in a stronger way. We need a democratic republic, support for trade, import of raw materials and export of finalized goods, moral support, no humiliation (!), under all circumstances severe prevention of every kind of rearmament by an international authority without hope of relaxation.

'Would you, please, excuse my quite insufficient English!'

So writes a very able and distinguished German. He may write with an accent, but I submit he thinks the very best English possible. I would add to his 'no humiliation' – 'no false pride'. That is the phrase that I like least in his letter. The sooner we can have that German *It must never happen again*, written by Germans for Germans, the better for Germany and the whole world.

Heinrich Mann and the Committee of the German Opposition, and Professor Meusel of the Friends of the German People's Front in London, a monthly periodical, *Inside Nazi Germany*, and the Free German League of Culture in London, are all hopeful intimations of the possibility of a German Renascence. We British and our friends in America have to crystallize out our ideas of world reconstruction in common with such allies. We have to bind ourselves permanently to France to allay the natural fears of France. In a little while we may have an *It must never happen again* League, including such people as President Benes and Jan Masaryk, French radicals, neutral thinkers, and particularly the best thought of America, working out the common idea of a *single new world order*, making that idea so clear and definite as to be a commanding prescription of what has to be done.

There is no time to lose if that body of constructive opinion is to come into operation. There is no time to waste. Do not wait for 'leaders'. Act yourself. Spread this idea of *world collectivization plus the Rights of Man*. We do not want 'leaders'; we want honest representatives and missionaries to embody that idea and carry it everywhere on earth. In a sane world the idea and the law will dictate, and we shall have no more use for personal dictators and ruling gangs. The politicians will come to heel when they realize that the wind is setting steadily in this quarter of the compass.

THE END

If, having read this book, you would like to join the fight to help keep Wells's words alive and cherished, please consider supporting the work of the following organizations, all of which are campaigning vigorously to save the Human Rights Act:

Liberty
liberty-human-rights.org.uk
[f] facebook.com/libertyhq
[tw] @libertyhq
P 0207 403 3888
Liberty House
26–30 Strutton Ground
London SW1P 2HR

Amnesty International
amnesty.org.uk
sct@amnesty.org.uk
[f] facebook.com/AmnestyUK
[tw] @AmnestyUK
P 0207 033 1500
Amnesty International UK
Human Rights Action Centre
17–25 New Inn Yard
London EC2A 3EA

English PEN
englishpen.org
enquiries@englishpen.org
[tw] @englishpen
P 0207 324 2535
Free Word Centre
60 Farringdon Road
London EC1R 3GA